MW01068665

WICCA FOR BEGINNERS

Wiccan Traditions and Beliefs, Witchcraft Philosophy, Practical Magic, Candle, Crystals and Herbal Rituals

Dora McGregor

Wicca for Beginners

Written by Dora McGregor

First Edition

www.wiccantribe.com

Copyrights Notice

Limited Liability

Please note that the content of this book is based on personal experience and various information sources, and it is only for personal use.

Please note the information contained within this document is for educational and entertainment purposes only and no warranties of any kind are declared or implied.

Readers acknowledge that the author is not engaging in the rendering of legal, financial, or professional advice. Please consult a licensed professional before attempting any techniques outlined in this book.

Nothing in this book is intended to replace common sense or legal accounting, or professional advice and is meant only to inform.

Your particular circumstances may not be suited to the example illustrated in this book; in fact, they likely will not be.

You should use the information in this book at your own risk. The reader is responsible for his or her actions.

The information provided herein is stated to be truthful and consistent, in that any liability, in terms of inattention or otherwise, by any usage or abuse of any policies, processes, or directions contained within is the solitary and utter responsibility of the recipient reader.

By reading this book, the reader agrees that under no circumstances is the author responsible for any losses, direct or indirect, which are incurred as a result of the use of the information contained within this document, including, but not limited to, errors, omissions, or inaccuracies.

YOUR FREE GIFT!!

Thank you for adding this book to your Wiccan Library! To learn more, why not join Dora's Wiccan Community and **get an exclusive free spells book?**

Little Grimoire of Wicca Spells is a great starting point for anyone looking to try their hand to practicing magic and **include 10 beginner-friendly spells** that can help you to create a positive atmosphere within your home, protect yourself from negativity, and attract love, health, and prosperity.

Little Grimoire of Wicca Spells **is now available to read on your laptop, phone, tablet, Kindle, Kobo, or Nook device.**

To download for free simply visit the following link:

www.wiccantribe.com/freebook

Download WICCA FOR BEGINNERS in the Audio Book version for FREE!!

Did you know that all of Dora's books are available in audiobook format? Best of all, you can get this audiobook **completely FREE as part of a 30-day trial with Audible.**

Audible members receive free audiobooks every month, as well as exclusive discounts. It's a great way to experiment and see if audiobook learning works for you.

If you're not satisfied, you can cancel anytime within the trial period. You won't be charged, and you can still keep your books!

To download simply visit the following link:

www.wiccantribe.com/wiccabeginners

Table of Contents

Introduction

A Wiccan is someone who believes in the religion of Wicca who has knowledge of Pagans or follows their paths provided by Wicca. People who follow the Wiccan religion go by one saying which is very important: "Harm none, do what you will."

It states that if you are not harming anyone, then you are free to believe in whatever you would like and act as you please.

It does not force you to follow certain religious books and it does not include any supposed rules for you to follow. Wicca is all about teaching you how to allow yourself patience and self-care while being able to fully work on your spiritual and physical growth.

With Wicca, you can practice meditation and learn how to be self-aware while also being aware of what is around you. You can recognize what is unhealthy and make decisions to change.

Like Buddhism, Wicca helps you work solely on yourself and redefine your spiritual, mental, and physical being. Once you know your true self, you can develop further and will have the confidence to tackle whatever comes at you.

Chapter 1

The history of Wicca

Many of the traditions of Wicca come from more ancient Pagan belief systems and practices, however, the advent of Wicca and its founding philosophies originated in England and was introduced in the mid-1950s by a British civil servant by the name of Gerald Gardner.

A basic idea of Wicca is that it is considered what some might term Neo-Paganism, however, some distinct qualities and characteristics set it apart from the traditional denominations of the paganism practiced in more ancient cultures.

Before Gardner introduced Wicca to the public in 1954, the concepts of Wicca could be traced back to a woman named Margaret Murray who was a renowned folklorist, anthropologist and Egyptologist, who studied the traditions and cultures of a wide range of religious practices, combining a field study of these sects and describing in her own words the concept of witchcraft.

Murray wrote a large set of books about medieval religious practices, specifically those centered on witch-cults in Europe.

Her works inspired readers to rekindle the pagan arts by creating their covens, structuring their worship around the descriptions from Murray's books. All of this was going on in the early 1920s in Great Britain and Europe and likely led to Gerald Gardner's more structured philosophy called Wicca.

Gardener's book entitled *Witchcraft Today* demonstrated the origin of the word Wicca and what it means to the craft. In his book, it is spelled with only one 'c', as in "wica", and it wasn't until the 1960's that the second 'c' was added. Gardner mentions that the word 'wica' is a Gaelic, or Scots-English word meaning "wise people". He had always had an interest in the occult and eventually became initiated into a coven of his own in the late 1930s.

Eventually, he formed his coven in the late '40s, buying land and establishing it as a center for the study of folklore. It became his occult headquarters and where he would bring to light the Wiccan way through his writing and practice.

A great connection existed between Gardner and the famed occultist Aleister Crowley. The two men met in the late 1940s and had much to discuss their personal beliefs and magic.

Gardner's work and writing out of his rituals of Wicca for publication were strongly influenced by Crowley's work, which had dated back to the earlier part of the century.

Gardner published his works, one of them is a novel entitled, *High Magic's Aid*, which became one of his first standard tomes to describe the practice of Wicca.

It was his *Book of Shadows*, however, that became the most highly regarded and sought after. Gardner's Book of Shadows was his collection of spells, rituals, and other information about the craft. To this day, it is one of the most central books for the practice of Wicca, or at least for learning from the original Wiccan, Gardner himself.

Fortunately, Wicca was then, and remains to be, an ever-evolving practice and does not adhere to a strict set of rules.

It happens to be a very flexible religion and offers that people follow a simple set of ideas and concepts and that there is freedom within those ideas to explore and form a deeper understanding.

Initiates of Gardner's coven were given the Book of Shadows to copy out and use and that was one of the ways they belonged to the coven, sharing the same spells and rituals to carry forward and practice. Gardner met Doreen Valiente in the early 1950s before Wicca had it coming out.

She contacted him after seeing an article in a magazine about covens, witches, their practices, and what that reality was like. Under Gardner's guidance, she was able to revise *The Book of Shadows* for Gardner to offer it as a popular book for others outside of the coven and also prominent Wiccan circles, similar to how Crowley had marketed his beliefs and findings.

Valiente became a Wiccan leader of her coven and was a prominent figure and scholar in the world of steadily growing Wiccans. The story of Wicca, when you look at it like that, seems like no more than a trifle in the annals of history, but when you look a little deeper, it had a profound impact on the world of magic.

Leading up to Gardner's exposure of his new religion, there were several ways that people were still looking to practice the ancient Pagan arts. Witchcraft was an incredibly taboo practice and it was highly frowned upon for centuries after the witch trials.

The study of the past by Margaret Murray helped people to find a new appreciation and understanding for the beauty of this magic and if it wasn't for her work, and that of other occult philosophers, Wicca might not have been born. To be honest, it has always existed in some form or fashion and it has carried many other names. The big umbrella term for it would be Pagan, and that word houses a whole cornucopia of possible sects and denominations, practices, and rituals. So then, it begs the question: what makes Wicca different?

Based on nature worship of the pagan religions, modern-day Wicca approaches connection to the divine through rituals and practices, festivals of the solstices, observances of deities, specifically a male and female god form, herbalism, a code of ethics and a belief in reincarnation and an afterlife.

Some say that it is a modern-day interpretation of those pagan religions and traditions, which existed before Christianity.

It has its origins in Europe, but in today's world will also incorporate concepts from other religious practices like Shamanism and pre-Christian Egyptian religion. It has been noted that there are strong similarities to Druidism, as well, despite there being a lack of evidence about how the Druids truly worshipped.

A majority of Wiccans are duotheistic, meaning they worship a male god and a female goddess, or the Horned God and Mother Goddess, or Mother Earth. It is not always the case and even the early forms of Wicca, back in Gardner's day, were not strict. Most of the time, it was determined on a coven by coven basis, what deities would be worshiped by the group and how to perform certain rituals. Some other forms of Wiccan practice involve, and are not limited to, atheism, pantheism, and polytheism.

This opens the playing field to anyone wishing to establish a Wiccan practice, involving all of the other ethics and rituals into their work while getting the chance to determine how they want to worship.

The basics remain the same, but the deities or what gets worshipped changes. Apart from these components outlined in the earliest forms of Wicca, there is a devout appreciation for the Earth and all of her inhabitants which is why Wicca tends to be called a nature-based religion.

The use of herbs and plants in spell work and rituals is celebrated regularly, and also includes a devotion to the seasons of the Earth cycles and Moon cycles, bringing focus to all living rhythms.

The history of Wicca may feel recent; however, it comes from a long and green history of pagans, druids, witches, warlocks, and all of the individuals and covens along the way who had a sincere devotion to the presence of Earth magic and all of its gifts.

Giving attention to the origins of Wicca is an important beginning to your study and as you embrace the methods of how Wicca can be practiced, like those before you, you can build upon it to make it work for you the way that feels best. There are only guidelines and no strict rules. Wicca is meant to evolve with the individual, and whether you are practicing alone or in a group, the Wicca of the past will always be a part of the Wicca of the present. Your Wicca.

Wiccan Philosophy

Wicca can be described as a broad religion as it has the happiness of including a lot of different perspectives, realities, and beliefs.

There are, however, several major core beliefs that are practiced by a majority of Wiccans as a way to establish a grounding basis for understanding the magic you are working with when you are practicing.

These concepts are taken into account, no matter what coven you are in, or what deity you are worshipping. The concepts outlined in this chapter are the main platform, or foundation, of what Wicca is and how it explains itself to anyone wishing to follow this path.

Nature is Divine

A majority of Wiccans will tell you that nature is divine. It is like a backbone to the entire practice and there are so many ways that this core belief manifests itself in these rituals. We are all members of this Earth: every rock, tree, leaf, plant, animal, bird, insect, and person, not to mention hundreds of thousands of other species and landscapes.

The Earth is our sacred home and we are a sacred part of it. It is where all life energy is stored and recreated and we are a part of those cycles and systems. To worship nature is to worship the very essence of all things. And you will find that all Wiccan holidays and festivals that are celebrated are derived from the worship of nature.

Each festival is marked by a solstice or equinox. All esbats are marked by the cycle of the moon. And just about every ingredient in the rituals and spells of these festivities comes from nature somehow.

There is also a celebration like the unity of opposing forces. There is always a balance of the light and the dark and nature-worship provide the opportunity to look at life from that place of balance and serenity. It is the presence of the male and female in all things; the yin and the yang. That is nature.

The practice of devoting space and love to nature is a part of the Wiccan creed and even though it is not a demand that you follow that practice, it comes naturally when you consider all of the other core beliefs.

Many of the tools that you will use for your rituals and spells are derived from nature. You will find yourself gathering herbs or pieces of wood for making a wand. You may be harvesting certain plants to hang around your house for a certain holiday, or dressing your altar in the perfumes and trinkets of the forest floor. All of nature comes into Wicca and it is a powerful process to fully connect with the divine in nature.

Karma, The Afterlife and Reincarnation

Karma is an echo of what you may find in the Threefold Law (see below) which states that what you do in this life carries over into your next one. To make such a suggestion, one must believe in the concept of reincarnation, which creates an open doorway for your spiritual being and essence to return to another life, after your last one, to continue to learn lessons and acquire knowledge for the evolution of all things.

According to Wicca, this is what will always be and has always been, and so to adopt the principles of Wicca, you must look into the reality of who you were before, and who you are going to be next. It might be that you are already familiar with some of your past life experiences and you already know what lessons you are trying to learn from those lives. In other cases, for some, you gain new knowledge as you go and are not always privy to what you are supposed to be learning.

The concept of Karma asks that you remind yourself what you need to heal from your former lives so that you can ascend further into your true power and magic. And while you are at it, in this life you are living now, be sure that what you do is something you want to take with you into the next life. This also pertains to the Wiccan Rede 'harm none' (see below).

Although there is the concept of reincarnation, there is also the concept of the afterlife, sometimes referred to as Summerland, and it is here that you rest between lives to prepare for the next one, to gather your strength and reflect on the journey before to create the best journey forward.

All of these concepts help the Wiccan to bridge the gap between Earth and Spirit and that the balance of the divine is always present, no matter what life you are living, or what stage of travel you are in between worlds.

Ancestors

It is not uncommon to call upon the ancestors in the practice of Wiccan rituals and casting. Many Wiccans believe that our ancestors are always with us, guiding us and showing us the way and should be honored for their commitment to forging ahead and living life.

Wiccans celebrate deities of various kinds and it is normal to include your ancestors in your practice just as frequently, as they are a part of the cycle of the self and have many lessons to teach as you grow and honor your path. The concept of honoring the ancestors in not specific to Wicca and is a cross-cultural truth, present in most religious practices.

A great deal of worship for the ancestors comes from a need to embrace the past as well as what your ancestors continue to do for you in the future.

Wheel of the Year

All of the cycles of the year are celebrated in Wicca. Every solstice has a celebration or Sabbat, and every equinox, too. The rituals and spells that accompany these times are a sacred honoring and celebration committed to the end of something to hail the beginning of something new.

In the calendar of the year, some endless deaths and rebirths can occur and as a Wiccan, you will find harmony and abundance with every passing season because of that very truth: life begets death which begets more life.

In all of the seasons, there are also moon cycles that are celebrated throughout the ritual of Esbats. The cycles of the moon organize the seasons and every waning moon leads to an ending, into a darkening, while every waxing moon leads to a powerful fullness that has its magic and ritual associated with it.

All of the rhythms and cycles are a part of Wiccan work and it will be a part of this world forever. The concept of worshiping the divine in nature goes closely with the wheel of the year and should be counted as a major component of Wiccan worship.

Personal Responsibility and Responsibility

This concept agrees with the Wiccan Rede and the Threefold Law. You are responsible for every action you take. Wicca asks that you are wise to your power because it might be more than you realize, especially when you are working with the sacred divine energies of all things and all life.

When you are practicing Wicca, you are becoming responsible for more than just yourself; you are using the energy of all life to celebrate and support the life you lead and everything you choose can have an impact on another. It is a wonderful way for you to be honest with the truth of karma as well because whatever you are responsible for in this life, goes with you forward into the next.

You are incredibly powerful, and Wicca helps you to embrace your internal power and life force energy; it also asks you to be responsible with your power and to harm none and do right by your actions and rituals.

Benefits of Wicca

Becoming a Wiccan means that you are dedicating your life to being a more positive and focused person. It means that you want to develop strategies to take care of yourself and understand how to be one with nature and everything that exists around you.

It's not just about magical spells or creating potions, but rather wanting self-improvement. There are many benefits to being Wiccan. Wicca and witchcraft emphasized using energy from the earth and nature and also bringing the sky and air energy back into the earth.

Being a Wiccan is about feeling as though you are one with the earth, with all living things surrounding and embracing you. It's a peaceful religion.

People who are not Wiccan or do not follow the Wiccan Rede are concerned with control, power, and domination of the earth. They don't think about living things and they don't care to.

They want money and materialistic things to make themselves happy and feel good. This type of mindset is destructive and is one of the reasons that when someone has everything, they still feel as though they have nothing. Most people feel as though when they get everything they want, they will be happy, yet there are Wiccans or non-Wiccans like Buddhists that have nothing and are happy.

This is because they have taken care of themselves and worked on who they want to be for themselves. They view the world as a matter of all living things being one, and they are happy with themselves.

They are at peace with the world and try to give back or give to others as much as possible because they have a sense of well-being. Acting in this way is what it means to be Wicca.

The main aspects of Wicca are what will save the world from human destruction:

- Environmentally friendly people - Aware of the earth. (What affects one thing, will affect all of us, as whatever we do will come back to us three-fold.)
- Responsibility - Your words and actions are no one else's fault, even if it feels like they are.
- Honoring our gods and goddesses which make up all matter and all living things.
- Self-respect, and respect for others.

If everyone lived by these principles, the world would be a much happier place. Nature would live on to survive for centuries more.

All living things would grow and flourish into a beautiful place where they want to be. There would be fewer problems and more help from our society. This is why Wicca is so beneficial.

Wicca is about improving oneself to feel beneficial to the community and their religion. Wicca teaches self-empowerment while offering others the support they need to feel good in their lives too. The wisest thing a Wiccan lives by is as follows: *"If it harms none, do as you will."* This means that you can do as you please as long as you are not harming Earth or anything or anyone

23

around you. Wicca is more about keeping to yourself while focusing on your happiness and goals and avoiding trying to convert others or getting them to see your side. Just live, forgive, and let go. Some of the greatest things about Wicca are as follows:

Wicca is not judgmental. It honors and worships divine femininity; everyone is neither male nor female because everyone is seen as equal and as one. The goddess is the center of everything while the masculine traditions offer accomplishments of the sacred gods - Horned God and the Green Man.

Wicca is nature and Earth-friendly. Wiccans believe that Earth is part of us, and we are part of the earth and all it has to offer. They celebrate food and the gods and goddesses for providing us with all we have, as many cultures are less fortunate. Wiccans have an undeniable connection to all life on Earth.

Wicca honors the physical. The body, the mind, the soul, food, sex, and the physical aspects of the world are all seen as sacred to Wiccans.

Wicca demands creative independence. When someone has come up with an idea for the religion, Wicca is too quick to put that into the religion itself. Everyone is open to their creativity, and nothing is set in stone. Wicca has a strong need for poetry, songs, art, inner experiences, etc. It leaves room for mistakes and does not judge anyone for their past, or for who they are today. It's about self-love and inner peace.

Wicca cultivates family time and close bonding. The celebrations like Easter and Christmas are traditional in the fact that they bring families together and help them bond better. Thanksgiving is about appreciation for one another and about giving back to others. Wicca is not a dark religion, nor is it moralistic.

When they hear the name Wicca, right away, many people think about magical spells and Witchcraft. These are the people that don't know much about Wicca and judge based on what's said or what they have heard. Although Witchcraft is part of the Wicca religion, as you have read, it is not everything; however, there are many benefits to the Witchcraft side of things as well.

The Benefits of Witchcraft

No two people, or rather witches, are alike, and no two spells are the same. Witchcraft is all about the energy you put into your spells or potions and not the physical kind of energy. Wiccans are usually light witches and don't practice dark magick due to the law they stand by, which is to harm none. Here are eleven benefits to practicing Witchcraft:

Anyone can become a witch. People from all religions, backgrounds, and cultures can practice magick. Wicca is not the only religion that practices it, nor is it the only reason people will do Witchcraft. However, the reason most people think of Wiccans as witches or warlocks is that they are the most known religion that does practice Witchcraft.

No rules. As with anything or how most things should be in your life, you hold all the control. You can choose to make your spells; do your research about how to carry out certain things like protection spells or healing spells. However, you can make your Witchcraft as simple or as dynamic as you would like.

There are spellbooks and grimoires out there to help you, there are also guides and tools for you to mix when learning. Whatever you do though, be careful in how you use your energy because that is the main ingredient. When you are calm and peaceful, your spell will always turn out the way you would like it to.

It also doesn't matter about the lunar phases on when your spell will become successful or when you should start. Wiccans use the lunar phases as a guide to doing their own thing.

Anytime and anyplace. When you get good at Witchcraft, you can make up a spell or chant inside your head anywhere you would like at any given time you feel is appropriate. Wiccans and other witches have designated and sacred places to perform their spells and magick. But the choice is up to you on where you would like to learn, create, and spellbinding.

Nature spending. A ton of spells require certain herbs and also things you may have not heard of before, and so you will be spending a lot of time in nature learning about the balance of the earth. With practice, you will learn how to ask for permission and be able to hear the wind or feel the trees and soil beneath your feet. Witchcraft is about being aware of your surroundings, developing a strong mind through meditation, and understanding respect for all living things that involve your environment. There is no better place to get peace other than by yourself in a natural setting.

Knowledge. If you want to do something right or get something perfect, you will have a lot of studying to do. You will find yourself learning about herbs, flowers, roots, teas, potions, spells, and things you didn't think were possible. You will gain knowledge about natural healing, chakra healing, meditation, gems, crystals, myths, history, and the magical properties that every living thing holds. The more you know, the more powerful you will become, and the better off you and your Witchcraft will be.

Knowing what you want. If you are unsure about your passions or your journey as you truck through life, Witchcraft can show you and teach you things you never knew about yourself.

Spell work requires you to have a clear state of mind and a peaceful presence, and so when you do your spells, you have to make sure you are clear on what you want to happen here. As a successful process, doing spells and learning more about Witchcraft will give you insight on yourself and how to reach your most desired goals.

Distress or. Practicing Witchcraft is a time where you can focus your mind on what you are doing rather than all the other things life is trying to throw at you. It creates stability within your brain and your soul spirit. Witchcraft helps you reflect on what you have done, and where you are now for the sole purpose of getting your spell right and having it become successful. If your mind is cluttered, so will your spells.

So many paths to choose from. There are many witches including the sea witch, a hedge witch, a green witch, etc. Each witch has their unique specialties and practices their Witchcraft a certain way. With the many witches or choices, you have, you can find one that you can relate to with the most, and go down that path. Or you can choose all the paths and see what kind of witch you will be in a few years. The options are endless, and the choice is all yours.

Excuse celebrating. The summer and winter solstices are one of the many reasons a witch or warlock will choose to celebrate. For example, at the winter solstice, you may have chosen to be a sea witch (works with water), and create spells to replenish the Earth or soil in the dead months. The many Sabbats are easily celebrated, and no witch misses an opportunity to do their traditional rituals. These rituals may include preparing a feast with certain herbs and natural ingredients, go on nature walks to clear their minds, meditation to open their spirit, honor their ancestors for guidance, and many more.

Inclusive. Witchcraft can be anyone, it doesn't matter if you are bisexual, transexual, masculine, or feminine. This culture or religion surrounding Wicca is very "everybody friendly." No witch or warlock feels the need to judge, but they will feel the need to support and encourage. It allows people to try whatever they have wanted for so long and also promotes kindness, self-love, balance, and internal healing.

Increases healthy habits. Because Witchcraft uses everything natural, the teas they drink, the food they make, and a lot of time that they spend outdoors promote healthy habits physically and mentally. Witches spend their free time journaling their adventure, reflecting upon others and themselves, connecting with elements, and taking care of the Earth. They don't make excuses for why they can't do something, and when they have hurt someone unintentionally, they try to express themselves in a way that decreases the conflict.

The bottom line about the many benefits of Witchcraft is that in reality, your main practice is being in touch with yourself while being completely connected to Earth. It's about learning more about yourself and overcoming those unhealthy habits to set yourself up toward your goals. By reading and researching Witchcraft, you may come across many spells and techniques that are most comfortable with what you connect to.

By going this route, you won't be let down, or find any disadvantages, as Witchcraft is about making mistakes, and then gaining rewards and success from learning from your mistakes.

It is an empowering path to choose. With these many benefits comes the power of the mind. With nature comes the health of mental illness. Anxiety is released and mood swings dissipate. As long as you continue to strive for yourself, you will succeed in whichever path you choose.

How to Deal with the Public If They Don't Accept Your Faith

A lot of times, people will judge the unknown or what they don't understand. They may see you as weird or idiotic because you believe in the magick of Wicca. The thing about this religion though, is that as it is helping you feel more empowered, it will also help you with your self-esteem. When your emotions and mind are in check, what others say you can and cannot do is none of their business. There are two ways to go about your faith in Wicca, both are for many reasons. One way is that you could hide your faith, put your Wicca books away, and don't tell anyone.

The reason for this is you would be afraid to get fired, lose custody of your children, or be discriminated against for your practices. You may keep silent about your given religion because you don't want to indulge in who other Wiccans are as well and ruin their lives.

However, this could stem from paranoia about your faith and how people would act. The other way is to be proud of your faith, and whatever happens, will happen. You may choose to bring out those books, display your gems and crystals, and give advice or support to those who are down the same path as you. Choosing this route is a freer way to be.

Some things to keep in mind is to never ask someone about their religion if they are a Wiccan, some people may find it offensive, and feel judged. If they bring it up, you can show that you are open-minded to the idea, and even ask questions about it.

Also, if you happen to overhear someone's thoughts or faith about Wicca, never indulge or "out" them to anyone else, as it is never anyone else's business. It shows respect for the opposing party as well because you don't know if they want to hide it or if they don't care.

In addition to keeping Wicca a secret, many people choose this route because the person likes to preserve their power and energy, and also Witchcraft should be taught by another person, not by the public.

This is because Witchcraft should never be used for the intent to harm, and a true Wiccan will know the intent of someone else while teaching them magic. The people who choose to share their faith openly have their reasons because it shows personal empowerment, and courage stemming from physical, mental, and emotional strength.

Some Wiccans may feel that hiding their faith goes against the religion itself which makes them feel limited to what they can and cannot do.

When you are honest about your faith and open to the possibilities, your craftiness becomes more effective, and you will develop self-confidence on a level you didn't have before.

However, most Wiccans choose both sides, they share their faith with close friends and family but don't openly admit it to the world. Whatever suits you and your needs best is your choice, as there is not a wrong choice in this.

As you read, research, and study about Wicca and Witchcraft, be aware that before you choose any route, you should get all your facts right.

Generally speaking, elder Wiccans suggest that newcomers should practice, and dive into this religion for about a year before disclosing any information about it.

Find out what suits you, find out what makes you happy, and what you do and do not like. That way, by the end of the year, you will have a better understanding, have more experience, and feel more comfortable about how you will come out about your religion.

Maybe try a bunch of different religions within a few years before choosing what fits you best.

Types of Witchcraft

Just like how Christianity has its denominations in the form of Roman Catholic, Methodist, Anglican, and others, so too does

Witchcraft have its own set of denominations. Let us look at some of the different kinds of Witches below.

Gardnerian

As the name suggests, these Witches follow the teachings and philosophy established by Dr. Gerald Gardner. In this system of belief, witches practice the religion through a hierarchical system.

At the top, you have the high priest or priestess, followed by many initiates. To become part of the Gardnerian tradition, newcomers have to learn the traditions of the Witch, and then they should have gone through the right initiation process.

Alexandrian

Alexandrian witches follow their system of beliefs and practices. They also have their unique system of initiation and apart from sympathetic magic, they also make use of ceremonial magic. Alexandrian witches also make use of the Qabalah.

Solitary

As the name suggests, solitary witches are those who are not part of a coven. They prefer to practice Witchcraft and perform rituals by themselves. People might choose to be solitary witches either by their own choice or because they were never initiated into any coven.

Additionally, Solitary witches may incorporate the principles of different Witchcraft traditions (such as Gardnerian and Alexandrian) or they might not use any of the traditional beliefs and rather forge their path.

Eclectic

A Witch becomes Eclectic when he or she pulls from different traditions and belief systems to create the rituals and spells that he or she practices. Their witchcraft practice is more personalized as it involves the traditions of various cultures.

Their system of witchcraft is also prone to change or evolution as they incorporate new ideas and practices.

Traditional

When someone looks back into history and tries to draw inspiration from it, then that which becomes traditional by nature.

These witches look at old grimoires, historical backgrounds and accounts, and lore to create their practices and rituals. Because the history of Witches is different in various regions of the world, so are the type of Traditional witches based on the location they practice their craft in.

Hereditary

These are witches who have received their lessons, beliefs, and rituals from previous generations. Usually, these witches are born into a family of witches who has been practicing the art for some time.

However, a common misconception here is that just because someone is born into a family of witches, he or she automatically becomes more powerful than other witches. That is not true. We are talking about Witchcraft, not the X-Men.

Kitchen

A Kitchen witch is not one who has a large cauldron in the kitchen. Rather, they are a group of witches who turn their homes into a sacred place. Kitchen witches enjoy incorporating rituals into their cooking. They focus their energy on the food that they create.

These witches usually grow their vegetables and herbs. To them, the art of cooking is precious, and they care deeply about the meals that they prepare.

Cosmic

When Witches incorporate astronomy and astrology into their workings, they become known as Cosmic witches. These Witches closely follow the alignment of the stars and planets. They heavily study the symbolism of the various astral bodies present in our solar system and beyond.

Green

You might have guessed as to what "green" refers to. In essence, Green witches work closely with nature. This does not mean that other witches do not have any relationship with nature.

Simply put, Green witches use the seasons and natural ingredients to create their magical accouterments. They also prefer to perform their rituals in the presence of nature as much as possible.

Hedge

One of the special traits of Hedge witches is that they work with the spirit realm. They often create a boundary called "hedge" that separates the real world from the spirit realm.

This hedge is a physical border, usually placed around a particular location or their own house. To enter the spirit realm, they simply have to exit the hedge.

Common myths and misconceptions surrounding Wicca and witchcraft

Flying broomsticks? Old ladies with green skin? Evil cackling laughter? Hansel and Gretel?

All myths.

And there are more. As we have seen, the church was responsible for spreading much of the rumors surrounding Witchcraft and you know what happens with rumors: they begin to take on a life of their own.

It's like a game of Chinese whispers. You whisper something to a person and ask them to pass on the information down the line. What the last person will hear may not resemble the original message at all. So, it might have started with an account by some person saying, "They leap into the air on broomsticks!"

That eventually turned to a proclamation that Witches "Fly into the air using broomsticks!"

We all know where that went. And so, in similar ways, much of the myth that you hear about Witches and Wicca is simply blown out of proportion. As in, way out of proportion to a point where you don't even know what the original shape was. So, let us look at some of the myths of Wicca.

Witches Are generally Evil

Let us begin with the mother and father of all myths: that Witches are generally evil.

Let's straighten this out if we haven't already. Witchcraft is one of the most peaceful religions you are ever going to encounter, and that's not because I am writing this book.

One of the main reasons that people use the term Wicca instead of Witch is because of the degree to which Witches were ostracized, attacked, and condemned. Imagine that.

You are condemned to such a degree that you decide to rename your identity and belief.

One of the important facts to note about Witchcraft is that it condemns violence and harm done to other people.

Wicca Is Ancient

While the theories, rituals, practices, and principles that guide Wicca are ancient indeed, the entire system was a recent creation.

It started with the Father of Wicca, Dr. Gerald Gardner himself. He combined both folklore and traditions with modern belief systems to create a whole new set of practices, rituals, and beliefs.

Wicca Is Not a Religion

The United States courts declared Wicca as a region in 1986.

Witchcraft is Satanism

Not even close. When people began to choose apostasy (the act of leaving a particular religion) to worship the Devil, the church blamed Witchcraft for the situation.

If you had to compare Wicca to any religion, then you can compare it to Hinduism for the sole fact that it involves numerous deities.

Wiccans Sacrifice Animals

That is the opposite of what Witches and Wiccans believe in.

Witchcraft respects nature and everything else that is offered by nature. This includes both the flora and the fauna. Plants, flowers, insects, animals, and even the soil beneath our feet are considered sacred by the Wicca.

While it is true that Wiccans make offering to their deities, these offerings are generally in the form of bread, wine, special scented candles, minerals, and other non-meaty items.

Wiccans Have a Dark Bible

The Book of Shadows is not a Dark Bible!

It is simply a collection of rituals that the Witches put together along with other information that they think is important for them to remember.

It is a ritual book and a reference guide all put together. If you had to make it simple, then the Book of Shadows is a journal for Witches.

Chapter 2

Wicca in our modern world

With the creation of various rituals — whether they were for fertility, for growing crops, for success in hunting or better weather conditions — there arose a necessity for someone to conduct the rituals. This individual would be well-versed about the beliefs, deities, and requirements of the tribes.

These individuals were thought to bring better results when conducting rituals.

Dr. Murray had the belief that in many areas of Europe, these priests became widely known as the "Wise Ones" or Wicca.

Although this statement is often debated (not the fact some priests were called Wicca but about how widespread the name Wicca was initially), what is known is that in many Anglo-Saxon kingdoms, kings and rulers would not make important decisions without consulting with the Witan (derived from the name Wiccan, used to refer to a single wise person where Wicca denoted a whole group of people).

The Witan was labeled the "Council of Wise Ones."

Eventually, the level of importance of the Wicca began to rise. These priests had to have a thorough knowledge of not just magic, lore, and divination, but also of history, medicine, and politics.

 They were not just priests, but close advisors to the king. In other words, a mere whisper of suggestion into the ears of kings could send two factions into a state of war. Indeed, priests began to hold considerable power.

To the general public, the Wicca were the mouthpieces of the gods. But when it came to performing rituals, the same Wicca were considered as equals to gods.

Then Christianity arrived.

The Growth of Christianity

Many people believe that Christianity involved a mass conversion but that was not the case. In fact, during its early stages, Christians came under heavy persecution. Both Jewish and Roman leaders targeted Christianity for numerous reasons.

After a great fire broke out in Rome in the year 64 A.D., the emperor Nero came under heavy criticism. He needed to shift the focus of attention away from himself or risk being deposed (or backstabbed by someone you know. It was Rome after all).

He found the perfect scapegoat in Christianity. What made his campaign of targeting the young religion even more successful was the fact that back then people already harbored a misconception about Christianity. Many Christian rituals were thought to include acts of cannibalism. Others were considered to encourage incest.

The stage was practically set for anyone who wanted to blame Christianity for some calamity like, say, a great fire. Through such events, Christianity had slow growth, but it still found a way to spread vastly.

Eventually, an attempt was made by Pope Gregory the Great to mass convert people. To make this happen, he made the people build churches in the same spot that older temples and places of worship were established. It was as though the old religions were being removed and overthrown by Christianity.

However, the pope did not exactly receive the results that he wanted. You see, people were not as gullible or as open-minded to the presence of a new religion as he had hoped. During the time of the construction of the first Christian church, the only stonemasons, artisans, and labor available were people who were "pagans," a term referring to anyone who practiced a religion that was not Christianity. While decorating the churches, these pagan workers added symbols and designs of their religion into the structure. These little additions were done cleverly, in a manner that would escape the scrutiny of Christian priests.

But since Christianity was slowly growing, Wicca and other pagan religions were its opposition. There are, of course, many ways to get rid of opposition. You could sit down and have a proper conversation. You could discuss various logical steps that each party can take to ensure the harmonious existence of both entities.

Or you could do what the Christians did: turn the belief systems of the opposition into something nefarious and sinister.

The church focused its efforts on shifting the perspective of the people about the so-called "Old Religions" (a.k.a. Wicca and other pagan beliefs). Their main focus was to show that these Old Religions worshipped the devil. Hence, the very image of the Horned God was adopted into Christianity as a symbol of the Devil.

Lo and behold! A devil with horns was born (or created, depending on how you look at it). When the idea of the Devil became rooted in the practices, a singular, most obvious conclusion was drawn: paganism involved devil-worshipping! Eventually, this idea of the Devil and paganism became a staple of the religion. As the belief endured, so did its ability to permeate into every section of society.

If you were to count the number of movies that showed witches as people who are conjuring demonic presences, haunting the woods (come on, we have "The Blair Witch Project" and its many sequels to prove that), or simply creating mischief to unsuspecting humans and compare that to those movies that show witches as people living in the woods, then you might notice the difference.

Many missionaries and priests in parts of the world have used the rhetoric about pagan worshippers and the Devil.

But I digress. Back to the Horned god.

In those days, during the growth of Christianity, it did not matter what kind of people followed Wicca or whether they lived much happier and fulfilled lives than Christians. As long as they were practicing a faith that did not include Jesus, they were shunned from society or were asked (asked being a polite term) to convert.

The Devil Wears Nada

According to Professor Henry Ansgar Kelly of the University of California, Los Angeles (Biography.com Editors, 2014), the Devil is mentioned just three times in the Old Testament. Even during those appearances, the Devil performs actions that are administered by God. That doesn't seem like the evil king of hell that we all know about.

Here is another fact to consider.

The whole idea of "evil" being attributed to the Devil is a result of a mistranslation. In the original Hebrew version of the Old Testament, the word for the devil was Ha-Satan and in the original Greek version of the New Testament, the word used was Diabolos, both words meaning "adversary" or "opponent." There was never any separation of powers when it came to dealing with religion.

Because there was an all-loving and all-good God, there was just the need to create an entity to give the people the idea that their misdeeds are not going to go overlooked. After all, if God decided to suddenly toss people into eternal fires or make them carry boulders forever, then it doesn't sound like the actions of an "all-good and all-forgiving" entity. They needed another manager for that department.

Even the views of monotheism (the idea that there exists only one God) was not developed by Christianity, Judaism, Islam, or any of the religions that we are familiar with. It was an idea born in Ancient Egypt, during the reign of Akhenaten.

The goat was a symbol of the Horned god. Nowadays, anything connected to the Devil or dark arts use the goat as a symbol.

Begone Heathens!

As Christianity grew, the Old Religions began to fade away slowly. Much of the practice of Wicca was conducted in the outskirts of the countries. There were very few people who would openly declare themselves as part of the Wicca belief. The words "pagan" and "heathen" were then used to describe anyone who practiced the Old Religion, which is not a bad thing.

Surprised? I bet you are thinking that I just went over the edge, that I am about to tell everyone how terrible Wicca is. Not even close. You see, the word "pagan" is derived from the Latin word "pagani," which translates to "people who live in the country." Essentially, it was used to refer to Wiccans, Witches, and anyone who practiced the Old Religion.

Additionally, the word "heathen" is also Latin, translating to "one who dwells on the heath." Heath is a word that describes an open and uncultivated land. Some define it as an area that resembles the countryside. The terms were more descriptive of the nature of non-Christians when they were first used. All ideas of the two words being derogatory are a modern construct and quite incorrect.

The Campaign Against Witches

It was not a good time for anyone to believe in anything that did not conform to the ideas of Christianity. There was a spread of an anti-witch smear campaign, mostly propagated by the churches.

It did not help that Witches and Wiccans did not practice their religion openly, creating an air of mysticism around them. Additionally, the fact that they included rituals that did not involve just singing hymns and praising the Lord turned them into outcasts.

Everything that the Witches did was used against them. Witches used to perform rituals of magick to promote fertility and improve crop conditions. The church claimed that it was because of these rituals that women became barren and that crops were not healthy. There was no mention of the idea that if Witches were indeed responsible for the actions they were accused of, then everyone would suffer equally. Anyone who raised the point was silenced immediately under threat of persecution. One of the rituals performed by the Witches to improve fertility involved participants to head out to the fields during a full moon.

They would then use long tools such as poles, pitchforks, and broomsticks and ride these tools like riding toy horses. They would circle the field and chant, asking the gods to grow the crops with much health. The followers would leap as high as possible into the air. The higher they jumped, the taller they wanted the crops to grow. This was a form of sympathetic magick that did not have the noblest of intentions, but a harmless ritual.

To the church; however, this was an opportunity to turn the idea of Witchcraft on itself. According to the church, the Witches were working against the crops to destroy them. They were not leaping into the air, but rather flying on broomsticks and other tools. Surely such actions could only mean that these people were under the influence of the Devil!

Soon, the fear of Witches took hold among the masses. In 1484, Pope Innocent VIII used this fear to persecute Witches openly. It was two years later that two monks, Heinrich (Institoris) Kramer and Jakob Sprenger, wrote a book that dealt with anti-witchery.

The book was named *Malleus Maleficarum*, which translates to The Witch Hammer. Using the acts of Witches to brand them as evil, the book included detailed instructions on how to deal with Witches. At that time, the official censor (an official or a group of officials responsible for looking at works of art and declaring them as too obscene, politically motivated, or harm to society) was the University of Cologne. Upon reading the book, most of the professors decided that they did not want to be involved with the book at all.

Kramer and Sprenger, on the other hand, decided to use more nefarious actions to get the approval on the book. They forged an approval letter from the university, which essentially said that the work of *Malleus Maleficarum* was approved and even admired by many of the professors. The result was like bringing a match to a flammable substance.

There was mass panic and hysteria. People took to the streets to condemn Witches. Anyone who was even remotely suspected of being involved in rituals was brought to the streets or were turned over to the authorities. A sense of religious fervor and hatred against Witches took form, one that was not based on any rational thinking. This mood spread all over Europe.

For the next 300 years, Witches would be persecuted. No matter what violence was inflicted on Witches, it was deemed acceptable by the church on grounds of "removing evil." In some cases, inhabitants of an entire village were put to death because of the presence of just one or two Witches among them.

In 1586, the Archbishop of Treveres had concluded that the local Witches had caused a severe change in the weather, turning it into a freezing winter. By using methods of torture, a "confession" was obtained, which led to the rounding up of more than a hundred men and women. These men and women were then burned to death. As we had seen, fertility was an important part of Witchcraft. For this reason, certain sexual rites were also enacted by Wiccan. When the Wiccans were brought in front of Christian churches, they were asked to recount these rites in detail, much to the delight and amusement of the judges and members of the court. In the end, there was never an exact number to account for the people who were hanged, burned, or tortured by the church. But many estimates say that the total number is close to nine million people. Remember that not all of the people who were sent to their deaths were Witches. As the Witch trials spread across the region, it gave opportunities for people to get rid of anyone they harbored a grudge against or simply disliked.

A good example of how innocent people were caught in the persecution can be understood from the famous case of the Witches of Salem, Massachusetts. It was never confirmed whether any of the victims who were put to their death were followers of witchcraft or the Old Religion. Many people were outstanding members of the community and even the local church!

God and Goddess

Wiccans worship their gods and goddesses through critical awareness. They are aware of the following:

- There is only one "source".
- All gods and goddesses represent a variety of faces from the source.
- All living things on Earth are elements of the source.

The Wiccans' deepest loyalty is to their gods and goddesses which is the "one" behind the mask. The one is the thing you form all your devotion to. The most important thing in Wicca is that you *do* worship your gods and goddesses. The first rule in Wicca and the way of your life is in devoting and dedicating all your actions and your awareness to the creator - whatever that may be for you.

In any religion, they all have one thing in common which is to worship their one divine source. In Christianity, it is a higher power, and in Hinduism, they have many gods. In China, they worship the Jade Emperor. The gods and goddesses are the ones who share their lives with you and with whom you choose to share your journey. In Wicca, the deity is a transformational spiritual practice to perceive the divine as something that lives in every being as every being:

- Your Mother - the Goddess
- Your brother - The God
- Your baby - The Divine
- Your friend - The Source
- Your enemy - The One
- Your cat/pet - All that is
- Your self - The Eternal Light

The list explains that everything around you is your gods and goddesses. When you truly understand that the divinity is none above others is when you can fully begin to worship all that surrounds you. The list above is what the Wiccan deities are.

Chapter 3

The Wiccan holidays of the Wheel of the Year

Wiccans have what is called the "Wheel of the Year", and it is used to mark down all the major solar and lunar events, which are what their holidays are based on. For example, the Sabbats are for celebrating the sun's influence on Earth, which is the seasonal growing cycle. Wiccan Esbats celebrate the moon phases, especially the full moon.

Here is a list of the Wiccan Wheel Year:

Name	Holiday	Earth Event	Date	Occasion
Samhain	Halloween	fifteen' Scorpio	October 31st	Cleansing and releasing. Celebrating the dead. The Pagan new year.
Yule	Christmas	Winter Solstice	December 22nd	Rebirth.
Bridgid	Candlemas	fifteen' Aquarius	February 2nd	Purification, allegiance, and initiation
Eostara	Easter	Spring Equinox	March 21st	Innovation, revitalization, and new beginnings.
Beltane	May Day	fifteen' Taurus	May 1st	Fertility, happiness, and passion that fuels life.
Lithia		Summer Solstice	June 21st	Passage, and planning
Lammas	First Harvest	fifteen' Leo	August 1st	Appreciation, abundance, and fruition.
Mabon	Thanksgiving	Autumn Equinox	September 21st	Giving thanks, thoughtfulness, and expression.

On all these holidays and events, the Wiccan needs to do traditional rituals. Whether you do it in a group setting, in a quiet get-together, or a full-on drama ritual routine, the point is that you do worship and do the ritual. The rituals consist of:

- Honoring the divine in all the elements of life
- Recharging or regenerate your spiritual batteries
- Centering and balancing yourself with Earth's shifting energies.

The Wiccan dates are confusing, but to start a holiday or a "new day", the Wiccan dates start on the previous day at dusk once the sun has gone down. Each coven or witch will have their way of doing things, but most of the time, the holiday starts at sunrise on the date.

Sabbats and Esbats

Sabbats and Esbats are the time for regrowth, birth, or death of something. They are old traditions that have gone on for centuries, and thanks to our ancestors, they are the start of how our world works today. Eight main Sabbats are revolving around the sun; The Wheel of the Year starts like this:

Yule (Winter Solstice)

On December 21st, 22nd, or 23rd, "Yule" - the winter solstice - starts. Normal people would call this Christmas, and it is the longest night of the year. The festivities of Yule originated back to the Norse people for whom this time of year was for feasting, merrymaking, and, depending on what was believed, sacrificing.

The Wiccans celebrate by decorating a tree, caroling, drinking, and spending time with their loved ones. According to Julius Caesar, this was the time of year where the Druids would sacrifice a white bull and collected mistletoe for the celebration.

In Wicca traditions, Yule is celebrated from back in the Celtic legend of the Holly King and the Oak King. The Oak King represents the light of the new year, and the Holly King is the symbol of darkness. The ritual is when the Oak King tries to take over the Holly King.

Imbolc/Oimelc

This holiday falls on February 2nd and is the first of the three festivals when the Earth starts to replenish the goods. Egyptians thought of this holiday as "the Feast of Nut". Nut's birthday fell on

49

February 2nd and was seen as a mother figure to the sun God Ra according to the book of the dead. Nut took the form of a scarab beetle and, at the dawn of February 2nd, was known as Khepera.

Ireland converted to Christianity, and the church allowed them to worship the goddess Brighid because the Irish found it difficult to get rid of their old gods. Brighid is viewed as the woman aspect of the "maiden/mother/crone" cycle in Wicca and Paganism.

The ritual consists of leaving a piece of their clothing outside for Brighid to bless the day before February 2nd. People put out their fire and make sure the ashes are flat and smooth.

In the morning, there should be a symbol or sign that Brighid has left behind if she had passed by the campfire that was made.

If the sign is there, Wiccans would then bring their clothes back inside as they would then have protection and healing powers thanks to the blessing of Brighid.

Ostara

Depending on which day the spring equinox falls on, this day starts on March 1st, 2nd, or 23rd. This day is known as the second of the three spring festivals.

The word *Ostara* originated from *Eostre,* who is the Germanic goddess of spring. It's the same day as the Christian Easter celebration, and also what we would call Easter, and at this time, the Jewish Passover takes place. This holiday is one of the "new" holidays for Pagans and Wiccans because the Pagan Germans and Celts did not celebrate this holiday.

The March Hare was a symbol of fertility and growth in the medieval cultures in Europe; this is because mating season happens in March for rabbits, and they all come out in the day when they usually only come out at night.

Beltane

The third of the three spring festivals falls on May 1st, and it has been celebrated for centuries. It means that summer is right around the corner. This is when fire rituals happen, and it stems back to the Greco-Roman religions. It is a fertility month, and the Celts honored this date by giving their gods gifts and peace offerings.

Their cattle had to walk through the smoke of the balefires for fertility and health blessings. In Wicca, a Beltane ritual involves fertility symbols, including the Maypole dance. The pole consists of flowers and ribbons that are woven by the dancers.

By the end of the dance, the ribbons are intricately woven together to form a pretty pattern. May 1st first represents the endless circle of life bringing birth, growth, death, and rebirth to life.

Litha/Midsummer (Summer Solstice)

Depending on which day the summer solstice begins, this day falls on June 21st or 22nd. Many cultures have celebrated this day as the first day of summer, and it is a celebration to balance the light and dark. This day is the longest of the year, and it's when the sun reaches its highest point in the sky. Just as winter solstice had begun, the Oak King and the Holly King take battle again.

The Oak King is seen as the winter to summer solstice ruler, whereas the Holly King is seen as the summer to winter solstice ruler.

Midsummer, or Litha, is a time when Wiccans would light fires on high hilltops to honor the space between heaven and Earth. In other religions, it is a battle between light and dark.

On the first day of summer, the Oak King wins the battle for power, but by the end of summer and by the beginning of the winter solstice, the Holly King takes the power back.

Lammas/Lughnasadh

This holiday falls on August 1st, and it is thought to be the celebration of an early harvest. In some religions, this day is used for worshipping Lugh, a Celtic god of craftsmanship.

Lammas is the first of three harvest Sabbats and defines the time between late summer and early fall. In modern days, we do not understand the hard work and survival that our ancestors had to undergo.

For us, we go to the store to buy bread, and if we run out, we just return to the store. August 1st represents life and death for our ancestors, as they had to make sure that the first grain was cut, and then the wives had to make bread from scratch.

A lot of families would starve if the grain was cut too late or too early. This is a day to give thanks and recognition to our ancestors, as they are the reason we have food on our tables today.

Mabon

Mabon is what we call "thanksgiving", and it falls on September 21st or 22nd, depending on the fall equinox. It is a reminder to us that the long days and hot summer weeks are about to end, and the long winter nights are right around the corner.

This is a time when there is an equal amount of light and dark, which is why we give thanks to all that we have to our crops and harvest. We celebrate the gifts of nature and Earth, while at the same time coming to an acceptance that the soil is dying as the days get colder. In many Wiccan religions, this ritual consists of giving food and harvest to those less fortunate.

This time of year, is about the celebration of the harvest and kinship, but also about the balance between light and dark, as the darkness of the moon and the light of the sun are equally balanced.

Samhain

In modern times, we call this day Halloween, and it always falls on October 31st. This holiday goes back thousands of years, and it is known as the witch's new year. Witches will contact spirits through a seance because the veil between this world and the Otherworld is at its thinnest. The celebrations begin at dusk on the 31st, and the new year of the Celtics begins on November 1st, basically indicating that the old year has passed and a fresh new year is now beginning. This is because the harvest has been collected, the soil has died, cattle have been brought in from fields, the leaves have all fallen from the trees, and the earth is slowly dying around us.

This time of year, is about saying goodbye to the old and starting to make room for what's to come. For some religions, this night is when they remember their ancestors and all that they have done, so they celebrate their memory.

The Esbats revolve around the moon's cycles of lunar phases, and in these celebrations, modern Wiccans and Pagans celebrate the festivity with magick and by honoring their gods and goddesses. Covens usually meet once a month on a full moon to do healing magick rituals. All magick ceremonies represent when the moon is at its different stages - for example, full moon, dark moon, last quarter moon, first-quarter moon, and so on. If a Wiccan was to begin a project, they would start at the sight of the new moon and continue their process as the moon goes through the stages within the month. Generally speaking, a new moon to a full moon represents the beginning of things, and a full moon to dark moon is used for the death of things, like getting rid of the negative things from your life.

New Moon Magick

This moon represents new beginnings, and so this is the phase when witches would start a project. Offerings of milk and honey or water and fertilizer for the plants is how the witches would give thanks to their gods. The goddesses associated with this moon are Diana, Astarte, Artemis, and Ana.

Crescent Moon Magick

This crescent moon faces to the west to the gates of rebirth and death. The shape of the moon means the ladle of love, manifestation, and abundance, and it is the symbol of the goddess. The crescent represents the cup of the goddess' hand, which represents the gathering of information and new ideas. The goddesses worshipped in this moon phase are Aphrodite, Themis, the Celliech, and Tiamat.

First Quarter Moon

This moon represents growth and to build upon. So, when you see this moon, it is the time to put effort into what is holding you back.

Gibbous Moon Magick

This moon is 10-14 days after the new moon and is the perfect time to make the changes you need from the previous moon phase. It's time to either relax and take some time to think and regain energy or put forth energy into what you have been working on.

Full Moon Magick

The full moon allows you to predict the future and to protect yourself and the ones you love. Psychic powers are heightened at this time, and goddesses such as Arianrhod, Danu, Isis, Ashera, and Selene are called upon to come to help you at this time. Creativity is developed, and chances of success in what you are doing are greatly increased.

Last Quarter

If you want to rid yourself of bad habits, decrease illness, and banish negativity, this moon provides you with the strength to do so. The last quarter moon represents the death of something - to banish something from your life.

Dark Moon

This phase is the most appropriate time for dealing with faultiness or anything that is against you. You should call upon the goddesses Kali, the Morrigan, the Calliech, Lilith, and/or Hecate.

The Wiccan Elements

The elements involved with Wicca include air, fire, water, earth, and aether (which is defined as spirit). The elements are used for spells and are connected to every single thing that involves nature.

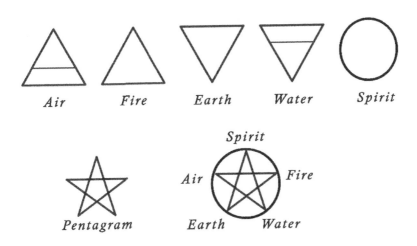

Each witch or practitioner needs to learn about and completely understand the attributes of these elements, which takes time and patience.

Air

In Wiccan magick and rituals, objects are tossed into the wind, aromatherapy is used, songs are sung, and things are hidden in really high places. The spells associated with air involve travel, instruction, freedom, and knowledge, they and can be used to increase psychic powers. Others things air represents are as follows:

The mind and intelligence

- Communication
- Telepathy
- Inspiration
- Motivation
- Imagination
- Creativity
- Dreams and passions

The symbols associated with the air element are the sky, the wind, the breeze, clouds, feathers, breath, vibrations, smoke, plants, herbs, trees, and flowers. The goddesses to call upon when doing air spells are Aradia, Arianrhod, Cardea, Nuit, and Urania; the gods are Enlil, Kheoheva, Merawrim, Shu, and Thoth.

Fire

In Wiccan rituals, witches will burn objects, use love spells, baking ingredients, and light a candle. Fire is the element of change, and it is the most physical and spiritual of the five elements. It represents the following:

- Energy
- Inspiration
- Love
- Passion
- Leadership

The symbols associated with fire are flames, lightning, heated objects such as stones, volcanoes, the sun, the stars, lava, and heat.

The goddesses to call upon are Brigit, Hestia, Pele, and Vesta; the Gods are Agni, Horus, Prometheus, and Vulcan.

Water

In Wiccan rituals, this is associated with pouring water over objects, making potions, healing spells, bathing, and tossing things into a bucket of water. Water represents the following:

- Emotions
- Absorption
- Subconsciousness
- Purification
- Eternal movement
- Wisdom
- Emotional components of love and femininity

The gods and goddesses to call upon are Aphrodite, Isis, Marianne, Dylan, Ea, Osiris, Neptune, and Poseidon.

Earth

In Wiccan rituals, it is common to bury things in the earth, create herbs, and make things out of nature, such as out of wood and stone. It represents the following:

- Strength
- Abundance
- Stability
- Prosperity
- Wealth
- Femininity

Aether (Spirit)

This element is the glue for all the other elements. It provides balance, space, and connection for the other elements. Aether is connected to our sense of spirit and well-being, and it represents joy and union. The goddess to call upon is the Lady, and the god to call upon is the Horned God."

The Wiccan Rede

The Wiccan Rede is what most Wiccans choose to live by. It is a statement that says harm to none, and do what you will. The word "rede" stems back to Middle English and it means advice or counsel.

Chapter 4

An Overview of Wiccan Covens, Circles, and Solitary Practice

Creating a Circle

A circle is a great way to create personal space for performing rituals. It also protects the Witch from any external influence. As long as you are within the shield, then no negative energy can interrupt your ritual or influence you negatively.

Creating a ritual is not a complicated process. Here are the steps you will need for it.

Step 1

Make sure that you find a quiet place for this. On the other hand, if you already have an altar, you can create a circle around it. If you feel that the circle cannot go around the altar, then you can create a circle in such a way that two points meet at the altar. That way, your altar itself completes the circle for you. You have to be prepared for this process. This means that there should not be any interruptions while performing this process.

Step 2

Find the four cardinal directions using a compass. If you already know them, then skip right ahead to the next step.

Step 3

For each of the directions, place a representation of the elements that they are attuned to. We have already discovered that the north is represented by the earth element. In similar ways, find the elements for each of the four directions. As for what the representation of the elements means, it could be any object that could be symbolic of that element. Here are some examples that you can use:

- Earth: crystals, rocks, branches, potted plants

- Air: incense, feather, a bundle of sage
- Fire: candles, an oil lantern or burner
- Water: bowl or mug of water, seashells

Step 4

Now stand up and look to the east. Ensure that your breathing is calm and steady. If you feel that you might need to meditate before this entire process, then I have provided a simple meditation technique that you can use in the next section. For now, keep your mind calm and grounded in the ritual you are about to perform.

Facing the east, imagine that the wind is blowing all around you. In a clear, but soft voice says, "To the spirits of the air, I seek your guidance."

Slowly turn to the south. Imagine the sun above you, throwing its warmth and heat to you. As you can imagine the power of the sun flowing through you, speak these words softly and clearly: "To the spirits of fire, I seek your guidance."

Now turn to the west. Imagine the waves crashing against your feet. Imagine the feel of rain on your body. Imagine how the water feels on your hands. Then speak these words clearly and softly: "To the spirits of water, I seek your guidance."

Turn to the north. Imagine the feel of the earth beneath your feet.

Or imagine the sand slipping through your fingers. Or you could even imagine how the earth feels when you touch it (this might be easy if you have been working with plants or trees). Then speak these words clearly and softly: "To the spirits of earth, I seek your guidance."

Return to the original position.

Note that if your original position was facing any of the directions, then you can come back to it. For example, if you started the ritual by already facing the direction of the east, then you will end up facing that direction. This does not have any influence on the rest of the ritual.

Step 5

Sit down crossed leg or in a position that is comfortable to you and begins meditating. Imagine the power of all the elements flowing into you. From you, they are flowing towards the circle and then powering them.

Step 6

When you are done (ideally, you should have meditated for at least 5 minutes), stand up. You are now going to thank each of the elements for their assistance.

Look to the east and say in a clear voice: "To the spirit of the air, I thank you."

Look to the south and say in a clear voice: "To the spirit of the fire, I thank you."

Look to the west and say in a clear voice: "To the spirit of the water, I thank you."

Look to the north and say in a clear voice: "To the spirit of the earth, I thank you."

Magical techniques like astrology, tarot, runes, and more.

There is a lot to learn about magick, but we will cover them in detail later. For now, I just wanted to give you a short introduction on what magick means in Witchcraft.

The first thing that you should know about magick is that it involves timing. If you have been reading about Witchcraft or of Wiccan beliefs, then you might have read or become aware of the fact that the moon plays a vital role in rituals. This is not a rumor that someone conjured.

The moon is indeed important in Witchcraft rituals. However, the misconception lies in the fact that all rituals are performed at certain times of the year. While the effect of performing rituals under certain moon phases does help in boosting the effects of that spell or ritual, you can perform the ritual or cast a spell at any time during the year. On the other hand, certain rituals are made specifically for certain phases of the moon.

Essentially, there are two main phases of the moon. When the moon shifts from the New Moon stage, go through the First Quarter, and enters the Full Moon stage, then this phase is called the Waning Moon. When the moon shifts from Full, Last Quarter, and then finally to New Moon, then this phase is called the Waning Moon. Think of it this way, when the Moon is increasing in size, then the phase is referred to as Waxing and when it decreases, it is Waning. These phases are related to sympathetic magick.

You take an object and resemble it to the ritual you would like to cast or the outcome you would like to have. In this case, the Waxing of the moon (increase in size) can be used to improve upon things.

Would you like to improve the opportunities in your life? Would you like to enhance the love that you and your partner feel? Would you like to have more friends? Any ritual or magick that focuses on increasing, enhancing, improving or other related results use the Waxing Moon.

On the other hand, you have the Waning moon. If you are aiming to reduce something, then this is the phase that is ideal for the ritual. For example, are you planning to reduce the negativity in your life? Are you planning to remove evil presence? Do you want to manage depression or other health issues? Then you can use this phase.

Each ritual is unique and can be performed during both phases, depending on how you create the ritual or what purpose you would like to achieve. For example, let us say that you have caught a nasty bug. You would like to remove it from your system using Witchcraft. You can do one of the following:

1) If you are in the part of the year where there is Waning Moon, then your ritual should be focused on removing the problem from your body.

2) On the other hand, if you notice a Waxing Moon outside, then you cannot wait for the next phase before conducting the ritual! It's not like the problem is going to take a vacation just so you can prepare yourself! In such scenarios, the alternative would be to *improve* your health. That way, you are simply focusing the ritual on working past the problem and focus on getting you better.

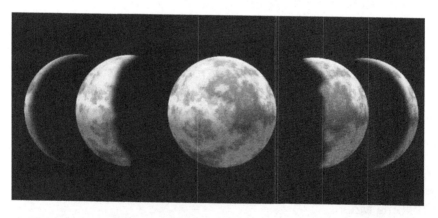

The phases of the moon play an important role in witchcraft rituals

The second factor that you should think about is that magick involves feelings. When you want a magick to occur, then you must be sure about the fact that you want the magic to happen. If you would like to get better, you must want it with all your being. You cannot decide that you are okay with it one way or the other and hope for the ritual to work wonders. It is for this reason that magick is usually performed on the self rather than on someone else. You can control your desires. You can guide the magick to achieve its purpose. On the other hand, controlling someone else's wants is a tricky thing. Your magick might not work effectively on them because they might not want it as bad as you want to perform the ritual. They might have changed their minds or moved on from the problem.

This "feeling" that you have is a sort of "power" for the ritual. You can enhance your power by using chants and rhymes. When you chant or loudly speak a rhyme that you have created, then you are essentially reinforcing the idea of your desires. In similar manners, many Witches also strengthen their spells by performing dance rituals or even having sex. Each one serves a specific purpose, depending on the spell you are casting.

Thirdly, one important note to make here is that when you are performing magick, then you should have a clean body. You have to clean your body both externally and internally before performing rituals. Why? Because you are asking for the favor of a god or goddess. It would be nice to show them that you respect the rituals. Here are the ways you can clean yourself:

1) To clean externally, take a bath with salts (ideally sea salt, but in the absence of that, you can use bath salts or regular salt). If you do not have a bath, then you can take a shower instead. However, make sure you try and use some kind of bath solution if you can get your hands on one.

2) To clean internally, make sure that you have fasted for at least 24 hours before you conduct the ritual. Abstain from the consumption of alcohol, nicotine, and other substances and sex.

Finally, and this is probably more of a guide than a rule. But before you perform any ritual, make sure that you ask yourself this question: Can your actions cause harm to anyone? If they can, then you shouldn't be doing it. No matter what happens.

Meditation and visualization techniques

Too often, you might find yourself plagued by numerous thoughts. When you are in such a state, you might find it difficult to attain a level of clarity. For such situations, here is a meditative technique that you can use. Firstly, find yourself a quiet place where you won't be disturbed.

You can either choose to sit cross-legged on the floor, sit on a chair, or simply lie down on the bed or a surface that is comfortable to you.

- When you are ready, close your eyes and take in a few deep breaths. You could use the counting technique to keep your breaths even and make sure that the time you take to exhale is longer than the time you take to inhale. So, when you are inhaling, count to five in your mind. Then hold your breath while you count to two. When you finally release, you can count to six or seven, depending on how long you take to exhale.
- Once you have taken a few deep breaths, return your breathing to normal. Just inhale and exhale. You don't have to hold your breath at this point.
- When you are in this state, you might notice a lot of thoughts struggling to get your attention. It could be a bad memory, a distracting idea, a future engagement, a project, or anything that is trying to wrestle away your attention from your meditation. Do not ignore these thoughts. Simply accept each thought as it comes.

- Let us say that there is a deadline for a particular project, and it begins to nag at your consciousness. Don't push it away, as it might return later and this time, with much greater force. Accept the thought. Don't think about why it is there. Don't worry about analyzing it or figuring it out. You are simply choosing to accept its presence. Once done, move the thought away and continue your breathing.
- You should be in this state for at least five minutes or until you find your mind in a more relaxed state.
- Once you are relaxed, simply take two or three deep breaths using the counting technique mentioned above and open your eyes.

You can always perform meditation whenever you feel that you might require it. You can do it each time you start a ritual or after you complete a ritual as well. Just a quick tip: if you are finding it difficult to sleep, you can use the above meditation technique to calm your mind.

The Magick of the Witch

Plant Magick

Throughout history, many plants (and I think probably every plant) have been used in Witchcraft to make rituals or in spellcasting. Some plants were discarded whereas others were used widely.

If you follow the concept of green Witchcraft, where plants are heavily used in the rituals, then there is a belief that all plants contain a form of the spirit. This spirit helps guide the ritual along (we had already seen this concept with animals and humans where each living creature has its unique spirit).

Now, why is it that plants do not have one spirit? Why are all plants not classified or managed by the same spirit? Simple. If cats and dogs each have unique spirits and they are two different species of animals, then it goes that plants also have unique spirits based on their species.

One of the things to note here is that you need to ensure you have awakened your inner Witch before using plants. More particularly, you need to follow the step that encourages you to spend more time with nature. This is because by being close to nature, you allow it to connect with you. Think of it like being in a social gathering. You see various groups in front of you.

If you do not mingle with these groups, can you say that you have understood them or know what is happening within a specific group? If you go ahead and join a group, then you get to connect with the members of that group.

You get to converse with them and understand them better. Eventually, you form bonds with the members of the group. The same theory applies here.

If you do not spend time with nature, how can you understand its powers and its essence? How can you connect with it?

When I say nature, I am not saying that you have to be in the middle of the woods. Go and spend time in a garden or your local park. Get potted plants into your home and then spend time with them. Head over to the nearest conservation center or garden your city offers you and spend time there.

There are many ways that you can spend time with nature. The important thing to note is not the "how," but rather "when." Try and make time for nature in your life. It benefits you in more ways than you can imagine.

Trees

In ancient times, the druids used to consider the trees as sacred. many of them performed rituals out in the open, close to the tree of their choice.

With that in mind, trees have their meanings and symbolism. And even though Witches and Wiccans often focus on herbs, it does not mean that trees are not included in rituals at all. Here are some of the magickal uses of trees.

Type of Tree	Magick Use
Ash	In many European cultures, ash is thought of as the World Tree. It is attributed to strength, strength, harmony, intellect, water, and skill. If you would like to create protection around your home or family, then you can plant an ash tree in your backyard or near your home.
Birch	Traditionally, birch was used to make many of the brooms used by Witches. It is attributed to the acts of purifying and cleansing.
Cedar	For non-magickal uses, cedar has been widely used to repel pests and insects throughout the ages. But magickally, cedar has been attributed to harmony, prosperity, spirituality, and the act of purification. You can also encourage abundance into your homes by building a cedar fence.
Elder	Elder is an ancient wood and is also known as "witch wood." Supposedly, people who do not ask for permission from the tree of an elder to use its wood suffer bad luck and misfortune. You have to use the power of threes while asking for permission or in other words, ask the tree three times to use the wood. There is

	no specific chant that you have to use. You simply phrase your question any way that you want to. For example, you can say: "Elder tree, may I receive permission to use your wood?" In the use of magick, elder wood is used for protection and healing.
Hawthorn	The haw translates to "hedge." It has been said that if the hawthorn grows next to ash and an elder tree, then fairies come out to dance among the trees. Magickally, this wood is used.
Maple	Commonly used for making furniture and other decorative items. Additionally, maple has also blessed the many pancakes around the world with sweet maple syrup. In the world of magick, maple is an equally sweet wood as it corresponds to love, health, life, and prosperity. You know, all the warm feelings stuff.
Oak	Oak is a plank of strong wood and is used in shipbuilding, homes, doors, and other woodwork. Magickally, oak is linked to courage, protection, good fortune, and long life.
Pine	The smell of pine is often considered as relaxing. You only have to walk in a pine forest to understand what we mean. Pine is often used in the manufacturing of cleaning products and soap to give that earthly scent. Magickally, pine is associated with healing prosperity and protection from negative influences or spirits.
Rowan	Another wood that falls under the label of "witch wood," is rowan, which is a favorite among Witches, especially in creating wands. Rowan is popularly known to have magical effects like healing, divination, protecting the user from evil, and improving psychic powers.
Willow	Willow is often connected to the goddess and feminine form. This is why it is preferred in those covens where the sole deity worshipped is the goddess. Magickally, the willow is known to bring about harmony, protection, love, and renewal.
Yew	One must be careful while handling this wood as it is poisonous. It is perhaps for this reason that the yew is associated with death. But while other traditions and cultures consider death as a grim subject to handling, Witchcraft simply acknowledges it as another step towards reincarnation. It is the end of one cycle and the beginning of another. Magickally, yew is connected to the spirit world.

If you had noticed, you were required to ask the elder tree permission three times before you could use it. While this might seem like a rule to follow for one tree, I recommend that you use this rule to pay respect to every tree you come across.

Not only does this ritual allow you to get the full power of the tree, but it also prevents misfortune affect you.

Why would you receive misfortune if you have not done anything evil? Think of it this way. If someone comes to your home, sits down at your dinner table, and enjoys your incredibly delicious and aesthetically pleasing lasagna, then the least they can offer in return is their gratitude. Imagine if they eat and simply leave your home without saying a single word.

You might not appreciate the gesture, even though you're willing to not make a big deal out of it. While nature is more forgiving and loving, it is still your responsibility to show your kindness in return.

Flowers

Flowers are essentially the sex organs of the plants. This makes it fertile and blessed by the goddess. As such, a flower contains a tiny bit of the goddess' energy within itself.

Flowers are an important component of natural magic. However, they can also be used in other rituals to decorate your altar or to create your spells. Here are some flowers that you need to know about and what they symbolize.

Type of Flower	Magick Use
Carnation	This flower possesses healing energy and can be given to those who are sick or recuperating from some injury. Magickally, carnations are attributed to luck, energy, strength, healing, and protection.
Daffodil	You can use this flower to make charms, especially for your loved ones. This is why, daffodils are magickally attached to luck, fertility, and love.
Gardenia	Another flower that is used in a talisman of love or alternatively. You can use it as a healing charm. Magickally, it is used in healing, tranquility, and love.
Hyacinth	These flowers possess a wonderful scent and are often used in homes. Magickally, they are associated with protection and happiness.

Iris	Witches often use this flower to attract blessings and to purify their spaces. Magickally, they are attributed to harmony and peace in relationships.
Jasmine	Often used in meditative rituals and as a scent, magickally, these flowers attributed to prosperity, spirituality, and love.
Lavender	The aroma of lavender calms the mind, body, and soul. It is often used to bring sleep to those who have difficulty finding it. Magickally, lavender is associated with healing, peace, and tranquility.
Rose	The flower of love! If one does not know what flowers to get during Valentine's Day, then the rose is the fallback option. While folklore (and fiction of course) has popularized the rose as a symbol of love, it has many more uses in magick as it is associated with peace, divination, healing, and spiritual growth.
Sunflower	Because the sunflower is associated with the sun, it is a symbol of vitality and good health. Magickally, it is attributed to success, happiness, and of course, health.
Tulip	Tulips are made to attract abundance and prosperity. This flower is associated with love, money, and happiness.
Violet	You can combine violet with another flower such as lavender and place in under the pillows of children to keep the nightmares away from them. Magickally, these flowers are associated with fertility, luck, love, and peace.

Herbs

Herbs are used in abundance in Witchcraft rituals and spells. Even if trees and flowers are not used as much, herbs are one of the essential ingredients in Witchcraft. Here are some herbs that you should know about and their magickal properties.

Type of Herb	Magick Use
Allspice	Allspice is commonly used in cooking and is an important part of a kitchen spice collection. Magickally, this spice is attributed to healing, love, and luck.
Basil	Basil is used heavily in cooking to not only add a slight flavor but an incredible aroma. Magickally, basil is attributed to peace, protection, success, and love.
Cinnamon	Cinnamon is a unique spice used in a variety of dishes. Magickally, it is used frequently to make charms and spells for love, vitality, success, and money.

Dill	Dill is also another herb commonly used in cooking. Magickally, it is associated with passion, protection, and prosperity.
Ginger	Ginger is an important spice in cooking. When it comes to magick, it is used to encourage romance, and improve the finances of a person.
Mint	Mint is an easy herb to grow in the garden or your own home. When used in magick, it promotes fertility, success, and purification.
Nutmeg	One of the more recommended herbs for solving problems with digestion. Magickally, nutmeg is attributed to money, love, and happiness.
Parsley	During the times of the ancient Greeks, crowns were made out of parsley for victors of various sporting tournaments and other reasons. This herb is commonly attributed to passion, strength, and purification.
Rosemary	One of the more unique uses of this herb is to darken the hair and cure itchy scalps. Magickally, it is attributed to memory, wisdom, and protection.
Sage	This herb is popularly used for protection. However, it has other magick uses such as health, wisdom, and protection.
Yarrow	A common garden herb whose magick properties are attributed to healing, courage, and love.

Crystals and Gemstones

Crystals are also used heavily in Witchcraft not just for performing rituals, but as decorative pieces. You can use them on your altar or create fashionable jewelry.

Crystals focus the energy directed at them and help you make use of that energy. Alternatively, they are even considered to store energy. Here are a few crystals and what they are attributed to.

Type of Crystal	Magick Use
Agate	Agate attracts good vibes and helps you manage your money if you are having trouble with that. Magickally, it is attributed to determination and strength.
Amethyst	This gem is used in meditation to help you enter a relaxed state. Magickally, it can be used to enhance your psychic abilities and call for divine assistance.

Bloodstone	One of the reasons people have this stone near them is to attract wealth. However, it has other magickal uses where it can attract courage, success, and good fortune.
Calcite	This gem is available in a variety of colors, allowing you to use it as a decorative piece in numerous ways. Magickally, it is attributed to healing and purification.
Diamond	A popular stone used in weddings and engagement rings and ceremonies. Diamonds are also possessive of magickal properties. It is attributed to courage and strength.
Emerald	Witches have used emeralds in clairvoyance. However, they have magickal properties that allow them to boost love, healing, and strength.
Fluorite	When placed in a room, this crystal helps remove negative energy in the air. Magickally, it is attributed to concentration, mental clarity, and intuition.
Garnet	Back during the Middle Ages, this gem was often kept in person or worn as jewelry to repel demons and evil spirits. Magickally, it is attributed to passion, love, and courage.
Jade	This gem is used to attract prosperity but has other magickal properties where it attracts good health and long life.
Malachite	One of the main features of this gem is that it attracts prosperity. However, magickally, it has many other uses such as attracting healing and then strengthening the connection with nature.
Moonstone	Shamans have used the moonstone to recall dreams. Apart from that incredible ability, this gem has been used to increase intuition, calm emotions, and improve health conditions for females.
Obsidian	In mythology and ancient lore, obsidian was the material used to create scrying mirrors. Remember the witch in Snow White who kept looking into her mirror and asking, "Who's the fairest of them all?" It can be assumed that the mirror was obsidian too. Magickally, it has been attributed to strength, protection, and for removing mental blockages.
Pearl	This gem is considered sacred to numerous goddesses. It is commonly attributed to fertility and creativity.
Ruby	When you want to improve sexuality and love, you keep a ruby around you. However, it has also been known to build courage and calm emotions.
Sapphire	This gem is commonly used to understand signs and omens. However, when it comes to magick, it is attributed to insight and wisdom.
Tourmaline	This stone is available in various colors

Chapter 5

Self-initiation techniques

It isn't enough to just say you are a Wiccan, because there are so many paths to explore, and which journey you choose to undergo is up to you. Many newcomers may become confused with this process because most religions only have one path with strict guides to follow.

No matter which you choose, what you have read up to this point is solely based around the religion, and how it has come about and why it is known for what it is today.

Every Wiccan still share the same views, celebrate the same holidays, and worship the same Gods and Goddesses.

First, you must understand what a coven is. It is a group of witches and warlocks who sometimes come together and are often very closely bonded with one another. Covens gather together to perform rituals, celebrate Sabbats, and practice Witchcraft on Esbats, as well as worship together at ceremonies.

A group of three or more is considered a coven, but most covens try to reach thirteen people. If a coven becomes too large in numbers to be manageable, they often split or break apart. Wiccan covens are generally led by a High Priest and Priestess, or one or the other.

Other covens may have a vote to switch leaders, and everyone inside the coven gets a turn at leadership. So, you have done your research and decided you wanted to become a Wiccan.

You have engaged in all their beliefs and lived by the religion through thick and thin. Eventually, you decide that it's about time to find other Wiccans and join a coven. But how?

This can be a tricky process because much like yourself, other witches or Wiccans have probably kept their faith a secret and shared it with other close relatives or friends. When finding a coven or other witches like yourself, you must use caution. Just like any group or set of people, there are good and bad, in this case, light witches and dark witches. Some use white magic while others use dark magick and will know that you are a newbie.

They may act nice and become your friend, but they intend to use you and steal your power to become stronger themselves.

Do not get the "dark witches" confused with the Wiccan religion. The witches who choose to use dark magick are not classified as Wiccan believers and do not fall under the name Wicca.

With that said, any Wiccan who practices dark magick is not Wiccan at all and are witches who practice black or dark magick.

As stated before, a true Wiccan lives by the following motto: "Harm none, do what you will." If dark magic is used, the witch practicing is not following the only true rule in Wicca.

Here are a few things to keep in mind during your search for others like you.

- Don't be desperate. The more anxious you are to find a coven or a witch the more at risk you are at finding someone who wants to take advantage of you.
- Get to know the opposing party first.
- Find out about their beliefs, what they have practiced in the past, and what drives them the most.
- Ask them about what they expect from you if you decide to join them.
- Do some research about the path these other witches have chosen. Learn the advantages and disadvantages (the goal is to be one step ahead).

- Before joining their coven do a public ritual with them to get familiar with what they do.

If it feels good, seems good, and there is a close bond, then it's probably good.

Although, through your journey of being a Wiccan, you may have experienced a deep intuition. You must always listen to your instincts. If things feel good, then do it but ease into the group and gatherings, never rush. There are some signs of coven cautions in which you should run away from or avoid at all costs.

The last thing you would want is for a dark coven to take your light from you because they seem to know what they are doing.

However, I would like to mention that if you do come across a "dark coven", they are not acting as true Wiccans. It is so important to realize what Wicca stands for and anything that portrays darkness is not Wiccan. Here are some coven warning signs in which you should stay far away from;

- Insists you obey their rules and laws while also telling you what you should think and feel.
- It makes it known that their way is the best and only way, which they claim to have the highest power.
- Demands that you believe what they believe and to forget everything you know
- Gets judgmental or even violent when you try to explore other options and learn from other sources.
- When you question them or their motives, they become angry with you or intimidating.
- Pressures you into doing things you don't believe in or are uncomfortable with. Says that you have joined the coven whether you intended to or not.
- Uses magick for dark things like trying to harm people and other living things
- Tries to convince you that dark is better than light.

- You feel as though you are not equal and need to earn your way to the top in their eyes.
- Wants and expects you to recruit others into the coven
- Says things like "I could get in trouble for teaching you this but..." or "No one else knows about this."
- Talks about summoning demons or controlling the Otherworld
- It leaves you with fear, shame, guilt, anxiety, and other negative feelings.

These are just a few signs that you need to be aware of, but mostly pay attention to your intuition and use your head when finding other covens. If something doesn't feel right, most likely it is not.

During your search, it is not just a good thing to watch out for the "bad" covens (non-Wiccan practitioners), but to keep in mind and be aware of the "good" covens as well. When you understand the key differences, you are ready to find what you are looking for.

Most of the time, finding a good mentor or coven is common-sense. Here are signs to watch out for when you have been introduced to a "good" mentor and coven.

- The teacher respects your needs and boundaries
- If the teacher asks you for a small but fair fee to teach you
- If they share their beliefs and interests with you
- They are patient, knowledgeable, and willing to share their expertise
- They are open, upfront, and honest
- If you find a teacher, it should be that they have been practicing for at least five to ten years
- Honor your right to seek out other sources as well
- Do not pressure you into anything
- Usually, leave you feeling confident, empowered, and motivated

- Their knowledge and ways of teaching are encouraging and helpful

A good indication that you have found a good mentor, or coven to join is when they make you feel good about yourself and treat you as an equal. In any case, though, make sure you never give your power to anyone. Ask for the guidance help of your Gods and Goddesses and follow their signs which should lead you to the right people.

Getting back on track to how you can find yourself a coven to join or a mentor to trust there a few steps you need to take to get there. Here are the steps:

Know what you need to look for

The first step is to have a clear vision as to what you need and want. Know what you are looking for before you start looking. Make sure your research is up to date and you are knowledgeable about what to find. A few questions to ask yourself are as follows:

- Do you need a coven? Why?
- What ideals are the most important to you? (look up Wiccan Philosophy for ideas.)
- Why do you want to practice Wicca? What would you use Witchcraft for?
- Why do you want to find others like you? To connect with, to talk to, learn from, or practice with.
- Once you have a clear vision of what you are looking for, you can start

Become known

The second step is to let yourself become known to other witches and covens out there. Let them know you are looking for help, and what kind of help you need. There are a bunch of spells and rituals you can do to "put out a call." After this, let the universe take over, and be patient as you wait for a response.

Take classes

The best way to seek out other witches is that you go into the world and take self-care workshops. Things like how to find what you want. Anxiety and mental health groups are good finds. Also, you may try looking into miscellaneous workshops that seem as if no one would take them but they still interest you.

Be found

The next step is to be found and be upfront about who you are (if you are comfortable). When you identify yourself by wearing Wiccan jewelry, then another witch may spot you and want to reach out. For a more subtle approach, wear things only other Wiccans would know about but that are classy or just unique designs to a normal person.

Seek other Witches

The last step is to find them yourself. Witches are everywhere, but no one knows who they are because they are still very private. The good thing about having practiced Wicca on your terms is that you are experienced enough to know the signs of someone else practicing as well.

- Go to bookstores, and observe what books people are reading. If someone is reading a Wicca book or spell book, then this can be a clue.
- Go to a witchery store, many towns and cities have them. These stores mainly have tarot cards, palmistry teachings, astrology, energy healing, crystals, etc.... You may run into someone. Yoga classes are good classes to sign up for. Many people who practice yoga, practice meditation, and

so when you meet someone, they may just open up to you about why.

- Sign up for Witch forums, there is tons of information online and with online witches. Who knows, you may even find an online tutor who can point you in the right direction.

If you decide to give up the search and just start your coven while having others find you then make sure you have done all your research before starting. You wouldn't want to come off as offensive or do things inappropriately because you don't know what you are doing.

If you keep Wicca Spirituality alive throughout your journey to start a coven or find one, you will always have the blessing and guidance of the Lady and the Lord.

Initiation

If you are a newcomer to Wicca and Wiccan beliefs, when joining a coven, you may be asking what exactly is initiation? What exactly do you have to do? The reason initiation is crucial is because, for some people, Wicca is just an interest.

Witchcraft and things to do with Wicca seem new and exciting but after a while, they lose interest. Others may just need to be introduced to Wiccan ways so they can discover their true path somewhere else. Then, there are those people who find a sense of peace and belonging to this journey that they have come across and discovered.

This is a way of life for these types of people. So, what is involved in a Wiccan initiation ceremony? First, you must figure out if you want to go solo or if you want a group with you that shares the same beliefs and values as you when it comes to this path.

When we think of the word *initiation,* we imagine some sort of group setting where a person is admitted into a particular organization. If you plan on joining a coven, then this image is almost correct. In Wicca, initiation means to pass down the knowledge of one Wiccan to another. In a coven setting, the leader will pass on their knowledge to the initiated, and when the leader feels as though the newcomer is experienced enough to do a ritual or practice on their own is when they are ready.

When the leader feels as though the "newbie" is committed to this spiritual path, then this is when they can officially join the Wicca religion or coven.

An initiation is different in every group; however, it is a process where a series of events helps the individual transform spiritually and is dedicated to this life decision. After this step, the individual becomes accepted into the rite itself.

One of the first steps, before initiation begins, is that the individual seeking initiation and the coven itself has to be wholly committed to each other. The individual has to find and be a good fit otherwise, it won't work out.

The initiated has to learn basic information involving the coven ways, history, and traditions to get a sense of whether or not the individual wants to contribute their energy to this coven.

When you do find a good fit, the next step is to work one-on-one with a mentor or leader of the group in which is called the study period.

This stage is when you become vulnerable, and share your beliefs and practices with the leader and vice-versa. Once initiated, it is your responsibility to commit to and honor your vows to the coven.

You will vow secrecy, attend meetings, and join every ritual to be a part of the coven membership. One thing is most important when seeking initiation into a coven or group. If you don't know what you are doing or looking for you should never enter.

Covens take initiation seriously and are willing to share their spiritual and emotional bonds with you while expecting the same. It is crucial that you are completely compatible with the group to avoid conflict of interest.

Most covens are closer to each other than their own families, so this is why it is very important to choose the right fit. It would be better to practice on your own than become involved and dedicated to a group that is full of conflict and is anything less than supportive and fulfilling.

Solitary Wiccans

A solitary witch or practitioner is someone who chooses to practice witchcraft in the privacy of their own home or another place that feels safe to them.

Many solitary witches prefer to experience things on their own and it requires self-dedication to their faith and spiritual path.

Although these types of witches do not have a coven, they may participate in the traditions of Wicca like Sabbats (holidays).

Many solitaries are called Neopagans which engage in the Pagan religions that include different forms of Wicca, Traditional Witchcraft, and many others. A solitary witch will teach themselves on the many practices and paths from Wicca.

They will read books, research herbs, and create their spell books. Aside from the many mistakes, one can make without guidance, they are some of the most powerful witches around.

One reason for becoming a solitary Wiccan or Pagan is because the individual does not want to feel judged or have to justify their beliefs to anyone else.

They fear that they may set themselves up for harassment or abuse within a group setting. Another reason for their choice to be solitary is that it is just their preference to practice alone because they feel more comfortable doing so.

With solitary witches, there are no initiation acts, but rather there is self-dedication to their practice and beliefs.

The solitaries choose this path because they feel it is right for them, and they don't feel the need to reach out to be initiated because they know what they want. Self-dedication happens when you declare a ritual or practice strictly to yourself and make vows to your deities.

You can call it whatever you like because in a sense it yourself that is fully committing to the religion and all of its practices involved.

You feel as though you are ready, and whatever you have been working on and researching, only you will know when you are fully ready to commit yourself to this path you have chosen.

So, whatever you decide to call this "self-initiation" process there are milestones to complete to fully commit.

Firstly, you must become familiar with the Craft - finding out what works for you, which witch you resonate best with, and which traditions feel most important to you.

The recommended time to study and practice this way of life is a year and one full day before self-dedication day. You can take longer, or if you are a natural, you can be shorter, but it must be something you want to do and are fully ready for.

The next step is to figure out what you will do for your ritual. You can find information online or in Wicca books.

Look for information, articles, or books called solitary practitioners for your best results. If you haven't found something you are interested in, then you may need to create your ritual, and by now - if you are truly ready - you should have enough experience and enough knowledge to design or create something like this for yourself.

Along with your research and pulling some pieces from here and there, when doing your initiation ritual, you may want to ask the guidance of your Gods and Goddesses to help you complete the process.

Initiation whether it is completely on your own, or if it is in a coven of your choice, is completely optional. With this in mind, understand that even though this is your choice now, it may and can change later. Some Wiccans have never been initiated and have practiced for years. There are also initiated witches who have lost interest and gone their own way.

If this is the life you choose, then you must acknowledge that you have to go at your own pace and follow your instincts to become completely successful in this religion.

Forms of Wicca and Wiccan Traditions

Along with the choices you can make about initiation, joining a coven, being completely solitary, or otherwise, there are decisions to make based around Wiccan traditions as well.

There are different types of Wiccans, just like there are different types of witches, which we will get into later. There are six different forms of Wicca and in each type, there are the traditions that they follow as well. Here is a list of the different forms and traditions of Wicca:

Gardnerism

Gardnerism is both a traditional form of Wicca and a family lineage.

The original book that was written by Gardener has been passed down, and there have been many versions. But within this Wicca form, the rules, or practices in this book are still preserved.

Gardner is largely responsible for bringing the first craft tradition to life. The Gardnerian Craft is the most familiar when we talk about Wicca and what Wicca stands for.

They hold the same traditions and undergo the same types of initiations; all covens hold a High Priestess or High Priest. They still follow the Wiccan Rede and are perhaps the oldest of the Wicca forms there are.

Alexandrian Wicca

The Alexandrian Wicca holds many aspects similar or the same as Gardnerian Wicca. However, the fire element symbol is an athame, and the symbol for air is a wand.

Alexandrian Wicca focuses mainly on the Holly King and the Oak Kings for several of their rituals and does much magick when celebrating their traditions.

The High Priestess is the highest authority of the coven and is usually a man that leads the group. Alexandrian is a bit different than Gardnerian because this Wicca is more diverse and socially formalized. Gardnerian keeps strict rules to refrain from nudity rituals, whereas Alexandrians leave it optional.

Mary Nesnick was initiated into both coven groups Alexandrian and Gardnerian. She implemented and combined both traditions and rituals into what is called Algard. The only way it was possible is that both forms of Wicca were so similar that it just seemed to work.

Dianic Wicca

The Dianic Craft involves two different branches. One branch was founded in Texas by Morgan McFarland and Mark Roberts. They honor the Horned God as the Goddess's beloved consort.

The coven is mixed with both females and men and is sometimes referred to or thought of as "Old Dianic." The other branch - branch two - consists of an all women's coven and is sometimes referred to or known as 'Feministic Dianic Witchcraft."

They experiment with different rituals and tend to be loosely structured. This group is supportive of an emotional and personal aspect.

Celtic Wicca (Church of Wicca)

The Celtic Wicca Craft was founded by two men named Gavin and Yvonne Frost. For a while, only the gods were honored and worshiped, but most recently the goddess includes their deity.

Celtic Wicca uses three circles using salt, sulfur, and herbs, whereas other Wiccans only use one circle. Unlike other Wiccans, the Celtic Wiccans insist on using a white-handled athame rather than a black one like everyone else.

The Frosts have gathered courses to teach about the Celtic Wicca and other forms of Wicca, which has been frowned upon, but is why they are more public in most of their traditions.

Georgian Wicca

Georgian Wicca is very dynamic and makes room for various styles and creativity. The best name for this group or Craft would be "eclectic." The founder of this Craft is George Patterson, and he used the phrase, *"If it works, use it - if it doesn't, don't."* This means that within the Georgian Wicca, as long as you do not harm, you can create and free your mind with practice whatever you want.

Discordianism (Erisian)

This Wiccan Craft is about orderly with the disorderly. So, in other words, the absurd is just as logical as the mundane, which is just as legitimate as chaos which, in turn, is as valid as of order.

Discordianism brings humor into the equation but should never be taken as a joke. It allows the practitioner to play games with an order, or games with chaos, or even both.

The effects of this craft on an individual can be exhilarating however, they may have missed spiritual growth together when joined with Discordianism.

Whichever path you decide to choose, you will find at least one that resonates best with you and who you are. These Wicca forms are not to define who you are or who you want to be, they are mostly about the history of Wicca and how it came to life.

What's more important is which witch you are planning to be.

There are hundreds of types of witches, and one of them is bound to suit you and your personality. The reason why it should take a year before thinking of being initiated is so that the individual can practice different spells according to each witch, and which suits them best.

Types of Witches

When we think of witches, we think of the old stories with broomsticks and the creation of potions and women cackling under the moon. This is the image of children's books or maybe the media of the old days have led you to think about witches.

However, this is not at all the case. The real story is that many types of witches are scattered amongst us. Below are some details regarding most of them:

Alexandrian witch. As we mentioned in 'Alexandrian Wicca,' it was founded by a guy named Alex Sanders and his wife Maxine. This is based on the ways of Gardnerian Wicca, but the main difference is that Alexandrian Wicca combines elements of traditional magick and Qabalah.

To become an Alexandrian witch, you must be initiated into a coven and obtain the three levels of Witchcraft.

Augury witch. The word 'augur' is a Roman term that refers to someone who seeks out to find out whether the Gods approve of a specific action taken by an individual.

The witches seek this information by translating signs and omens that the individual has experienced on their spiritual journey.

An Augury witch is a translator between the universal forces and people on a spiritual quest.

Ceremonial witch. The ceremonial witch does everything by the book. They have vast knowledge about traditions and rituals and most often will have grimoires and spell books.

They might have a book of shadows and draw on their knowledge such as sacred mathematics and quantum mysticism.

They call upon archetypal figures and understand spiritual entities that possess the kind of energy the Augura Witch wishes to have.

Dianic witch. This cult or coven focuses solely on worshipping the Goddesses and is more or less a feminist of all Wiccan movements.

The Dianic witch will honor their Goddess through three aspects containing, Maiden, Mother, and Crone. Dianic witches mainly consist of women.

Druid. Druids are perhaps the most secretive of all because there is not a ton of written information about them. Julias Caesar wrote about Druids in his diary *'The Gallic Wars,'* and described them and organized religion with their ways of doing things in rites and rituals.

Neo-Druids take their practices from old sources that originate from the Romanticism Movement of the eighteenth century.

Druids worship the Earth mainly revolving around nature, and implement these honors to their Gods through meditation and ceremonies.

Eclectic witch. Eclectic witches do their own thing and don't normally follow any religion or Witchcraft practice. Instead, they draw from their own 'higher self' and practice rituals or activities that work solely for themselves.

Most Eclectic witches have their practices and come up with their creation of rites and rituals that are derived from their research.

Faery witch. Similar to the Eclectic witch, the Faery Witch has its practices as well. The difference, though, is that they tend to have communication with faery folk and nature spirits. Many of their routines or Witchcraft is created from the individual.

Green witch. A green witch will communicate with 'Mother Earth,' by using sacred oak tree groves in their rites and rituals.

They do this because it brings them closer to nature and makes them feel closer to the Divine spirit. There are two different green witches in which they both use their materials for their ritual practices.

A Flora Witch will use flowers and flower materials for their rituals. An Herbal witch will use herbs and extractions from plants and minerals for their practices.

Hedgewitch. Just like a Shaman would be able to do, the Hedgewitch can travel to the Otherworld and communicate with the spirit realm.

This type of witch is known to be a powerful healer or midwife who specializes in delivering messages into real life to others and vice versa.

The word 'hedge' is a mark of a village or settlement in the old days where the boundary between physical and spiritual worlds was balanced.

Hereditary witch. The hereditary witch is a witch who has been born into a family of witches and brought up by their practices and beliefs. They pass their practices and rituals down to their children for generations.

The child who is born into this Witchcraft religion can still make their own choices and only become a Hereditary witch if you accept the practice into your heart.

Kitchen witch. A kitchen witch is not what they seem - brewing potions and cooking with herbs in the kitchen. They use realistic and useful tools to engage in rituals, ceremonies, and magic.

The Kitchen Witch enjoys decorating her home with magick and have it been a sacred and safe place to be.

Secular witch. A secular witch will use crystals, herbs, and stones in her practice; however, she does not define these items as divine or spiritual.

She believes that the objects she uses for her rituals and witchcraft activity holds energy and does connect to the universe and Earth, but the Secular witch doesn't worship any deities or spirits.

Solitary witch. The Solitary witch doesn't follow any organization or engage with a coven, and they don't belong to any religion or have a correspondence with any set practice.

It is said that solitary witches have practiced their craft for many lifetimes, and when they reach puberty, their knowledge is re-awakened.

This means that even though they don't remember being a witch, once they start Witchcraft, their mind does too, and so they are real naturals at it.

Thus, they don't need any help from anyone else to perform their magick rites.

Whether you decide to practice Witchcraft on your own, follow a coven for help, are already experienced, believe in Wicca, or don't.

The choice is purely up to you. You can be a witch without believing or worshipping any Gods and Goddesses, or you can be a full-fledged Wicca with your own beliefs and practices and create a bunch of covens together.

The choice is yours, as there is no 'right' or 'wrong' answer.

Awakening the witch within you

To awaken the witch within you, various methods combine both directly calling out to the powers to surrounding yourself with symbolic items.

Call Out to Your Power

Many had silenced the power of the Witches. You are going to call out to these powers. You are going to reach out to the god and goddess to grant you the power that was once taken away from Witches.

To do this, find a quiet spot. You can choose to be in front of your altar or you can find any other spot where you won't be disturbed during the ritual. Once you are ready, following the steps below:

- Make a triangular symbol with your hands by touching your thumbs and your index or first fingers.
- Now, slowly bring this symbol close to your abdomen area. Take a deep breath and exhale. You can even perform the

deep breathing exercises we had seen in the previous chapter.

- Set your feet apart and relax. Make sure that you are not feeling the tension in any part of your body. If you need time to perform a quick meditation, then you can do so before starting this ritual.
- With your feet apart, bend slightly at the knees. Close your eyes and bring your attention to the region of your third-eye. This region is located in the middle of your forehead, between and slightly above your eyebrows.
- In a clear voice, speak the words, "Oh God and Goddess, grant me the power that was once lost to me." If you have chosen to acknowledge only the goddess or god in your coven or practice, then you can change the chant above. You can say either, "Oh God, grant me the power that was once lost to me" or "Oh Goddess, grant me the power that was once lost to me." If you prefer, you can even replace the word god or goddess with the name of a specific entity. This allows you to directly connect with a deity.
- You have to repeat the above chant three times.
- Once you have uttered the chant, take a deep breath. Allow the power to manifest within you.
- Then speak this chant out loud three times: "I am deserving of this power."
- Finally, take another deep breath. Once you are done, speak this phrase only once: "Blessed be."
- Now you can relax and return to your original position.

Keep Symbolic Materials

You can always choose to keep crystals or other materials with you. We are going to look at crystals in-depth in the next chapter. But for now, let us look at the way that you can keep crystals with you.

- You can out all your crystals into a bag, especially a small pouch that you can carry around with you. You can either keep this push in your pockets or hand it around your neck.
- You can have a crystal bracelet. You can add as many crystals as you like in your bracelet or simply add multiple stones of the same crystal.
- A pendant is a stylish way to keep your crystal close to you. The best part is that you do not have to hide the pendant at all. You can choose to wear it openly. Some Witches even have different pendants for the various crystal to match their different wardrobes.

Surround Yourself with Nature More

Witchcraft is a religion that is based on nature. So, it would help if you headed out and experienced nature more. T

his could be anything from taking a walk in the woods or going hiking on a mountain to simply walking along the beach when it is relatively quiet. When you experience nature, you not only empower yourself more but also infuse your mind with positivity and calm.

Be Comfortable with Yourself

When you adopt the identity of a Witch, then any hesitation will diminish the powers that you have. This is because being a Witch means accepting everything about life. When you do, the god or goddess (or both) find it easier to communicate with you.

The best way to think of this is by using the example of swimming. Many people are afraid of drowning when they first get started.

But the idea is to face your fears and practice anyway. If you decide that you cannot do it and simply choose to avoid practicing swimming, then you will never learn to swim.

The same rule applies here. If you are going to be a Witch, then make sure that you are receptive to the powers of the deities.

And that can only happen if you accept yourself and accept them into your life.

Chapter 6

Step by step instructions for constructing a ritual

Rituals take many forms and represent so many different things to a Wiccan, or any person devoting themselves to this kind of magic.

Rituals have existed for as long as human beings have, even in their most Neolithic forms. The ritual is a cause to express intentions and devotions through the world of energy, elements, and spiritual connection and as you will notice in your research, every culture throughout history incorporates some kind of ritual practice into their lives. In Wicca, rituals are about the connection to the divine, spells, crafting, and honoring the deities and rhythms of life. They are specific to each practitioner or coven and can be delivered in a wide range of experiences and formats.

In your Wicca Starter Kit, you will have the step-by-step guide to performing a ritual. Keep in mind that each ritual must be altered and enhanced according to whatever magical purpose you are working with.

There may be a lot of ingredients for you to choose from and work with and there could be a lot of steps and degrees, or levels, of practice that you have to go through. It depends on your spell, and whatever steps you are creating through your Book of Shadows and your solitary practice.

If you are in a coven or choosing to become a part of one, many of the rituals performed are already outlined. This book focuses more on the ritual practices involved in a solitary Wiccan. Let's get started with these basic and simple guidelines to help you picture the process of your ritual work.

Step 1: Preparations

Before any ritual begins, you need to make the proper preparations for it. Preparations can include all or some of the following:

- Scheduling the ritual (Esbats and Sabbats have specific dates. Other rituals may need to fall on a certain date because of numerology, moon and sun cycles, birthdays, etc.)
- Organizing the steps (You will need to decide what order you need to carry out certain components of your ritual based on your knowledge of a spell you are working, or referral to your Book of Shadows. Having the information handy and in your cast, circle is an important part of preparing)
- Collecting your ingredients (You will need a variety of items, not including your altar or regular tools, that need to be used for your ritual. This can include specific herbs, crystals, candles, and their colors, types of incense, etc.)
- Bringing all of your tools and ingredients into space (You will need to have all of your collected tools, objects, ingredients spell book, or ritual instructions, and anything else you might need, in the space and ready to work on the chosen day and time)
- Setting boundaries with other life matters (You will need to turn off your cell phone and other distractions and create a time and space with your family and loved ones to give you undisturbed time to practice your ritual)

You may find other preparations outside of what is on this list and that is all dependent upon the specific ritual or spell you are trying to cast.

Step 2: Casting Your Circle

For every ritual that you perform, for the sacred quality and nature of this experience, you will need to cast a Ritual Circle to support the energies you are trying to engage with and focus on.

Follow the steps for Ritual Circle Casting in Chapter 4 to prepare your circle of protection. Make sure that all of your tools, ingredients, and objects needed for your ritual are already inside of the area you will be working in after your circle is cast.

Step 3: Honoring the Gods/Goddesses

Part of the reason people perform a ritual is to honor a sacred deity to their practice. Many Wiccans perform rituals for a specific God or Goddess and honor them regularly through a ritual to help them enforce their energies to work on other magical purposes.

The honoring of a deity or spiritual presence through a ritual is a sacred way to incorporate that presence int your everyday Wicca practice and will help bond you more deeply to the kind of magic you are choosing to practice.

Rituals open your space and your energy to receiving more of the gifts of that divine presence and so after you connect to casting your circle off protection, you begin your words of blessing and prayer to the god or goddess you are calling into your ritual, either to honor them directly as the purpose for the ritual or to include them in whatever other rituals you are working to perform.

Step 4: Tools and Ingredients

At this point in your ritual, you will likely need any tools and ingredients required to perform your ritual. You may have already used some of your tools during the casting of your circle and you will want to be sure to keep the tools you need to use in your ritual instead of using them for placement of the circle.

For example, rather than place your Chalice of water in the west, place a bowl of water there and keep your chalice in the center with you, or on the altar so that you can use it for your ritual.

Whatever herbs and ingredients you need to use can be prepared in whatever fashion they need to be. There are going to be specific instructions according to each ritual or spell and so you will need to have those instructions in the circle with you, to prepare your herbs and essences accordingly.

You will most likely be using your tools and ingredients together to complement each other's energy. This preparation stage can be on your altar or a table or on the floor where you are sitting.

Step 5: Connecting Your Intentions and Invoking Your Purpose

With your tools and ingredients ready to perform magic, you can begin the part of the ritual in which you will charge your tools and ingredients with the intentions and purposes of the ritual you are performing. You have read in Chapter 3 about how to charge and consecrate your tools.

Depending on your spell work and your intentions, you will imbue your ingredients, objects, and tools with that sacred purpose at this stage to prepare for the rest of the ritual. Putting that magical intention into your objects and tools first will only empower your ritual more fully and is an important step in the process.

Be specific and clear and let your intentions and magical purposes invoke the appropriate energy for your ritual.

Step 6: Practicing Magic

With your tools, implements, and ingredients charged and consecrated, you can now begin to practice your ritual magic. This stage will include a wide variety of steps and is entirely dependent on what your Book of shadows says to do, or whatever your spell work instructions might ask of you. Some of these steps can include:

- Lighting the candles specific to your spell (they will already be charged, consecrated and anointed if you followed the last step)
- Burning of certain herbs

- Using your tools in a specific way to invoke and honor specific energies and/or deities.
- Dancing
- Chanting
- Speaking Spell words
- Pouring specific beverages into the chalice to drink and honor a deity or holiday celebration
- Appointing certain elements to aid and guide you through the use of your wand or athame.
- Burning ingredients in your cauldron

There are plenty of other possibilities that will arise with certain rituals and spells. Some, none, or all of these things can occur on your ritual and it will be up to your Book of Shadows and your intuition to build the ritual and the steps involved.

Step 7: The Power of Words

This step will overlap inside of Step 6, as the words that you use for practicing magic will have a powerful impact on your ritual. You may say words during your ritual crafting and spells, but you may also have words to say after to empower and solidify your intentions and purposes.

Your words are specific to what you are celebrating and can be as simple or as elaborate as you choose. A sample of some words for a basic spell honoring the Triple Goddess on a Full moon ritual might be as follows:

Triple Goddess of the Moon, I honor thee with the power of three.
[light three candles, one for each aspect of the Goddess, as you speak the following lines]

Maiden sweet of springtime moon, I light this candle to honor you. *[light the maiden candle]*

Mother full of summer moon, I light this candle to honor you.
[light the mother candle]

Crone in depth of darker moon, I light this candle to honor you.
[light the crone candle]

Sacred Goddess throughout the year, on this full moon, I honor you here. *[light your Triple Goddess herbs with fire to burn in your cauldron]*

Bring to me your power of life, birth-death-rebirth, on full moon's light. *[pour wine, water, or another beverage into your chalice]*

I drink to thee, by power of three, to honor your sacred wisdom. [take three sips from the chalice, one for each aspect of the Goddess, with the next three lines]

To the maiden [sip]

To the mother [sip]

To the crone [sip]

By this full moon, I honor your vision.

So, mote it be!

Wicca is a creative practice and poetry of magical intention. Your words can be designed by your power and so anything you choose will specifically empower your spells and rituals to help you access deeper wisdom and scared connection to the great divine.

Plan out what words you will say before your ritual and have them available to read if you do not know them by heart.

Step 8: Closing Your Circle

Once you have performed all of the steps included in your ritual, you begin to close the circle. Use the same steps you learned in

Chapter 4 about how to close your circle and let your intentions carry forward into your life after your closing practice.

You may choose to decorate your altar with any of your ritual ingredients and you will want to organize your tools back on your altar so they can be ready for the next ritual you are planning.

After the Ritual

After your ritual, having returned your tools and ingredients, and closed your circle, you can now work with the energies you have called upon to help you on your path of magic. Your altar serves as a reminder to you what rituals you have performed and why keeping your intentions alive and your focus pure.

The energy of your ritual will only last for so long, and so you will need to decide when to move forward, clearing your altar of any remaining components of your last ritual practice. You want to keep your energy flowing, as is with all-natural rhythms in life.

Use your intuition to know when the powerful energy of your ritual has waned and when it is time to send that ritual forward into the next plane of spirit. You will know the more your practice and tap into your inner guidance as you perform more magic throughout your practice.

Practice

The practice is potentially the most exciting part about Witchcraft and Wicca. The practice consists of thing a witch will obtain and then use it in their rituals or ceremonies.

There are spells for all kinds of purposes and solutions. Before every spell or ritual, the practice takes preparation and a sense of knowledge about the intent behind the magic. Throughout this book you have heard and read the words 'magic,' and 'magick,' but maybe never knew the difference or what the individual words mean.

Magic with a "c" defines a method of manipulation into the physical world through metaphysical means by applying ritual activity. Magick with a "k" is a much more defined sense.

According to Aleister Crowley, who founded the religion Thelema and associated with modern occultism used the word as a way to differentiate the two. Magick with a "k" is different than magic with a "c" because it separates stage magic from Wicca and ritual magick. Crowley's primary reason for adding a "k" to the end of the word is that considered magick to be anything a person is moved by, and fulfilling their true destiny, in which he called "true will."

Crowley put a lot of thought into the letter "k". Magic is a five-letter word, but he needed it to be six, as six represents the hexagram - a six-sided shape. "K" is the eleventh letter in the alphabet which also held importance to Crowley. Six-sided shapes and numbers or words were influential in his writings as well.

So, in other words, magic with a "c" is for magicians who use tricks with cards and create illusions in the regular person's eye as a way to wow them. Magic, with a "k" represents the magick that is used in Wicca and spiritual practices.

Wiccan Ritual Preparation

With magick comes ritualistic practice. Witches will gather ingredients, pull energy from the Earth, and then make wherever their designation for practice is, suited for the occasion. Most ritualistic preparation stems from the Gardnerian traditions of Wicca or is used as a basic outline and setup. Each witch does their own thing, and each ritual is a little different but with many similarities to the following formula.

Purifying

The first thing witches will do to prepare for their ritual is to purify a circular area to rid bad energy or unwanted spirits. A witch will use a bristled broom to sweep the area, then burn sage above their head while walking along with the circular pattern. They will then pause at the north, east, south, and west sides of the circle. Every witch involved will burn sage and whisk it around their body.

Setting up the altar

On the east side of the circle, an altar is set with candles to represent the Gods and Goddesses. Also, on the east side, salt and water are set down for purification, then the athames of High Priest and Priestess, and finally incense. In each of the other four areas -north, south, and west - candles are lit and placed gently.

Casting the sacred circle

The highest members of the coven (or yourself) called the High Priest and Priestess will then cast the Sacred Circle. The circle is thought to be a spot that is without place or time and is cast by marking the edges with an athame or another tool, such as a sword, staff, or wand. They purify circle once more with salt and water, by placing three pinches of salt into the water and stir it specifically nine times with the athame.

The mixture is then sprinkled around the perimeter of the circle. Finally, incense is lit and carried around the circle.

Calling the quarters

Every witch (or just yourself) will then chant together calling the spirits of the four elements - Earth, fire, water, and air. These elemental spirits are guidance and protection for the witches.

Invoking the deity

A deity is needed for the witches to be able to perform magick, so the last step is to call upon them. Depending on the ritual, it can be a god, goddess, or both together. They are called by chanting out their names or reciting the gods and goddesses related to the ritual being done.

After this preparation is completed for the ritual, the witches will then begin whatever they were planning to perform. Once the ritual is finished, the ritual must end, which involves closing the circle.

To close the circle, you will do the same thing you did when you prepared for your ritual, only backward. The deities are thanked for their guidance and protection, the quarters are released, and the High Priests and Priestesses 'takedown' the circle. They do this by walking around the perimeter of the circle, opposite of the direction they started, with the athame pointed outward - away from them. Once the Circle is down, the witches help gather up the supplies and go about their days as normal.

The Tools Used in Rituals

Not all religions or rituals need 'tools' but most rituals do require them. In the Neopagan religion, various magick tools were used in their practice.

Each tool has its purpose and serves as direct magical energy. They are each usually established at an altar inside a Sacred Circle. In many Pagan traditions and Witchcraft, the witches will consecrate their tools before they use them.

To consecrate means to bless the items, they do this to purify them before they interact with the Divine, and also to rid the items of any negative energy that may be attached to them. In most cases, consecrating an item is a sure way to rid the tool of its history, so it is fresh and new with positive energy before you use it.

In other religions, the witches feel as though there is no need for consecration because whatever energy they are putting forth is already going into their tools, so consecrating them would only disrupt their energy flow. The bottom line, though, is that the choice is yours. There is a simple ritual in how to consecrate your tools, you can do this with jewelry, clothing, or the altar.

You consecrate it by offering the tool to the powers and energy of the four elements in which the tool becomes blessed in all directions. Many religions follow the same guidelines, but also have their ways of doing things for more experienced witches.

In the consecration ritual, you will need these ingredients, with each pointing in a certain direction.

- A white candle - Pointing south for fire
- A cup of water - Pointing west for water
- A tiny bowl of salt - Pointing north for Earth
- An incense - Pointing east for air

If your ritual consists of you making a Sacred Circle, it is best to do this now. Light the candle on the south side, and burn incense on the east side. Then, take the tool you are using or going to use, and hold it over the salt to the north and say:

"Powers of the North,

Guardians of the Earth,

I consecrate this wand of willow

[or knife of steel, amulet of crystal, etc.]

and charge it with your energies.

I purify it this night and make this tool sacred."

After this, turn to the East and hold the item over the incense and say:

"Powers of the East,

Guardians of the Air,

I consecrate this wand of willow

and charge it with your energies.

I purify it this night and make this tool sacred."

Next, it's time to face the South, holding the tool over the flame of the candle, being careful not to burn it. And say;

"Powers of the South,

Guardians of Fire,

I consecrate this wand of willow

and charge it with your energies.

I purify it this night and make this tool sacred."

Finally, turn to the West, and pass your tool over a cup of water and repeat:

"Powers of the West,

Guardians of Water,

I consecrate this wand of willow

[or knife of steel, amulet of crystal, etc.]

and charge it with your energies.

I purify it this night and make this tool sacred."

Return to your altar, point the athame to the sky, and repeat:

"I charge this wand in the name of Old Ones,

the Ancients, the Sun and the Moon and the Stars.

By the powers of the Earth, of Air, of Fire and of Water

I banish the energies of any previous owners,

and make it new and fresh.

I consecrate this wand, and it is mine."

Once you have done this with every tool that you intend to use, the ritual is complete. Not only have you blessed your tool or item for future rituals, but you have also claimed this item as yours.

When you do this, you are strengthening the energy inside the tool, and binding your strength with it. The great part about consecration is that if you have consecrated your main tool - a wand, athame, chalice, amulet, etc. you can use that to consecrate any item you need to in the future.

The question you may be wondering now is, what exactly are the tools used in rituals. It depends on what ritual you are practicing, and it also depends on the witches' preference.

However, for the most part, fourteen different tools can be used in any ritual. When first starting as a practicing witch or Wiccan, you may have the urge to go down to your nearest "witchy" shop and buy everything that you may think you will need.

The books you have read, and the study guides you have purchased all tell you that you need gems, crystals, wands, etc... the list goes on.

Although it is good to be prepared, every tool has its specific purpose and needs to be used appropriately. The following list should give you a sense of what you will need, and what you don't.

Every religion Pagans, Wiccans, or others have their tools and use all of them differently, so it is up to you to explore and figure out what you need most.

The Altar

The altar is usually found in the center of a Pagan ritual and is a table used to hold the tools you are about to use for your ritual.

You can choose to keep it up year-round or have a seasonal altar that changes as the Wheel of the Year turns. Some witches have more than one altar in their home normally represent their ancestors. The ancestor altar holds things like photos, ashes, heirlooms and passed down journals or books.

Other themed altars include nature or Earth altars which hold unusual rocks, or crystals, pretty seashells, and sand from different parts of the world. The nature altar may have chunks of wood or patterned flowers and wreaths for different seasons. The main purpose of an altar is to have your most valued items on there that suit the needs and purpose of you and your Witchcraft.

Athame

An athame is a tool many Wiccans and Pagans use for directing energy in their rituals and is often used for casting the Sacred Circle. The athame is generally a double-edged sword or dagger and is never used for actual cutting.

A bell

It is believed that loud noise drives evil spirits or demons away, which is what the bell is used for in most cases. The vibrations from the bell represent harmony as it includes, the shaking of a sistrum, a rattle, or the sound of a "singing bowl." In some religions or practices, the bell is used to start or end a rite, and to call a Goddess.

Besom

The besom is a straw broom and is used for sweeping a ceremonial or ritualistic area. Sweeping clears out any negative energy that may exist in the given space. The broom signifies as a purifier so it is linked to the water element.

Book of Shadows

A book of shadows is a Wiccan's or Pagan's memory or grimoire loaded with information. It generally contains spells, rituals, charts, the Theban alphabet, and the many rules of magick, plus much more. A Book of Shadows is a personal thing and should contain information that is most valuable and beneficial to you.

Candles

Candles hold many purposes and come in many colors. Besides just holding the element value of fire, and to call upon Gods and Goddesses, they are used in many spells. The idea behind the flame of the candle is that it obtains and holds your energy, while at the same time gets released into the atmosphere as it burns. In some religions, candles are thought to be more powerful if you make them yourself.

The Cauldron

The cauldron represents that of a chalice and is mainly feminine as it holds a womblike structure. The various ways you can use your cauldron for are:

- Burn incense, candles, or other offerings to the Gods inside it
- Use it with nothing inside to represent the Goddess of your ritual
- Blend herbs and other natural things for magical workings
- Fill it with water for moonlight scrying purposes

Cauldrons are not suitable for food if you are using them for magical rituals. If you are going to use a cauldron for food, make sure you have a separate one specifically for this purpose.

Chalice

Much like the cauldron, the chalice is also another feminine tool as it also holds the shape of a womb. It represents the water element and is used as a parallel tool to the athame in some religions.

This is so that together, the tools can represent the female aspect of the Divine during a token of re-enactment for the Great Rite.

There are different kinds of chalices and are often silver or pewter but all mainly act as the same thing. Some rituals have water put in the chalice and it gets passed around to other members of a coven during a ritual to bond or tie the witches together.

Crystals

Upon thousands of stones or 'crystals' that are out there, the purpose or intent behind your practice solely depends on you and which crystal to use for this purpose. We will talk more about crystal properties later in this chapter, but when using a crystal, it is best to pick one based on their attributes.

Birthstones also work great for the practice of magical workings and spells. Before using a crystal, it is best to cleanse it or consecrate it.

Pentacle

Most traditions and religions use the pentacle - not to be misunderstood by the pentagram - the pentacle is a flat piece of wood, metal, clay, or wax that has magical symbols engraved in it.

The most common symbol is the pentagram which is a five-pointed star. This is why the two terms are confused or mislead but they are much different. The pentacle is often used for protection, but in some Wiccan practices, it is seen as an element of Earth.

Robe

The robe is a piece of clothing, that when put on is a preparation for the ritual to begin. In some covens, you may have a certain color of the robe that you would have to wear. The color represents the level of witch you are or how powerful you are - just like the belts in taekwondo. The robe also presents your mind with a sense of stepping from the mundane world to the spiritual and magical one that you are practicing.

The Staff

The staff is not always needed, but many Wiccans and Pagans opt for the staff as it is associated with power and authority. In some coven or traditions, only the High Priest and Priestess are allowed to have one. The staff is considered male energy and represents the Air element

Wand

The wand is one of the most popular magical tools used in every tradition or ritual. The wand is used for directing energy and represents male energy, power, and masculinity. It uses the Air or Fire elements and can also be used to consecrate items or call a deity. The traditional wand is made from wood, but others are made from glass, copper, silver, and other metals.

Witches that do not use athames would instead use a wand for their rituals and practice.

A lot of these items you can make yourself; however, each tool has its special skill and ability for the purpose you are using it for.

Music and Magic

Music is used in Witchcraft or Wiccan practice because it helps call on spirits and Gods or guides to help with the ritual. Music is the language of spirit, and oftentimes in the religion, the instruments will be made from scratch with that of nature.

The natural sounds implemented in Wiccan practice is to raise powerful energy, alter consciousness, and connect you to deities.

Old day Wiccans created their instruments as a way to connect to Earth and nature. They would carve out the middle of a log to make a drum, found rocks that rang when hit, and flutes were made from bones and shells.

The main purpose of these instruments was to create sounds of nature such as the whistling of birds, the windy breeze, drumming of the rain, etc.

There has always been a hidden and deeper meaning behind the music that words can never explain. Music connects us to our internal selves and it gives voice to our dreams and desires. As music can help us connect deeper to ourselves, it also helps deities and powerful energies connect with us as well.

Instruments considered during your practice are:

Drums

The drum helps us stay grounded or connected when we are practicing a difficult spell or ritual. It is the representation of Gaia's heartbeat so the repetition of the drum helps us stay focused and come back to Earth if we need it. The drum is also useful for when we need to call upon the guidance or nurture from the goddess.

The Flute

The flute is a wind instrument that is directly associated with the Air element. Since the Air element represents intellect, these types of instruments are used to increase the witch's psychic abilities, improve knowledge, and find or possess wisdom. The Flute is used to call upon the god.

The Guitar

The guitar is a fire element and is used in spells and rites of sexuality, health, strength, passion, change, courage, and to get rid of bad habits. They are also used for purifying purposes so they will be strung or played before a ritual. The guitar helps to call upon the gods.

Resonant Metals

Resonant metals are things like gongs, cymbals, and bells. They associate with the most psychic of the elements, Water. Water represents healing, fertility, psychic power, friendship, love, and happiness due to its purification properties. The resonant metal instrument is mainly used to call the Goddess and is solely connected to nature.

These instruments are just a few tools that can be used before and during a ritual. Each instrument has its unique attributes to produce its power and that of a witch.

Spells

Wiccan spells are spell castings that are done by a Wiccan witch. Not all Wiccans practice magick, but the ones that do usually use the Book of Shadows for their guide. Spellcasting is about collecting your internal energy and power to direct it toward some sort of change in the world. Much like a ritual, spell casting can be done in different ways. Witches will draw energy from visualizing it, lighting candles, making herbal or crystal work, or by 'magical power' around them.

Any one person can cast a spell, but if you want it to work, it takes knowledge, practice, and concentration. You use your concentration on what your intentions are, become sensitive to your internal energy and the energy around you, and communicate with your 'Higher Self.' If you have not succeeded in doing so, then your spell may not work.

When casting spells, you need to understand the 'rules' of Witchcraft. These rules are set in place to protect you from accidental consequences and bad things returning to you. Consider reaching out to an experienced individual to help you, and guide you.

There are different types of spells like love spells, binding spells, and protection spells, for example. You wouldn't want to force someone to fall in love with you, so instead, you would use the love spell to have them shine more brightly than normal.

Because Wicca is about positivity, you always want to use the spell casting you are doing for good, not bad as you will want to be careful about the "Law of Threefold Return". So, if you intend to use a binding spell to get someone away from you, instead you would use a protection spell that will come in use.

When starting with spellcasting, it is so important to talk to someone experienced so that protection spells or whatever you try to do will work, and not fail unintentionally.

There are many protection spells however, most of them follow this formula:

You will need:

- A photo of yourself
- Four blue candles, or one white
- Essential oil for your astrological sign
- Sage for purification
- Three acacia leaves
- Three black tourmaline stones

The Spell:

- Wash your hands in a bowl of your essential oil and water, saltwater will work also.
- Prepare your Sacred Circle by placing a blue candle at the East, South, West, and North regions of your circle.
- Place the white candle in front of you

- To the left of the white candle, is where the incense is placed. To the right, would be the tourmaline stones.
- Place your photo in front of the candle
- Cast your circle and light the incense
- Pass your photo over the incense three times and imagine you being surrounded with purity
- Hold in your hands, the acacia leaves, and the black.
- Visualize yourself surrounded in a bubble of white light. Send your love, healing protection energies straight into this light to make the protection full.
- To end the ritual or spell, ground your energy, blow out the candles, and close the circle. Keep the incense burning until it is finished.

Spells can create positive change for you. Wiccan spells are to never harm you or someone else, and it can also protect you and the ones you love from harm. If the spells do not work, then you need more practice and are not experienced enough. Understand in-depth about the Law of Threefold before casting any spell.

Also, when doing Wiccan spells, you need to understand that none of it is dark, so it may not be as powerful as "black magick" but it's better than having darkness take over you.

Colors and Crystals

Colors mean many things and can boost your energy and power. Below is a table of the meanings of colors in Wiccan traditions. If any color holds a different meaning to you, then use your intuition and substitute when practicing.

Color	Attributes	What they are used for
Red	Love, bravery, strength, deep emotions	Love, physical energy, health, psychic ability
Orange	Energy, allure, vitality, arousal	flexibility to changes, motivation, power

Yellow	Knowledge, inspiration, creativity	Communication, trust, fortune-telling, study
Green	abundance, growth, riches, rebirth, balance	Prosperity, Careers, fertility, wellness
Blue	Serenity, truth, knowledge, protection, tolerance	Healing, psychic ability, peace in the home, sympathy
Purple/violet	Spirituality, knowledge, dedication, harmony, idealism	Prophecy, Enhancement of nurture abilities, balancing sensitivity
White	Peace, purity, enlightenment	Cleansing, clarity, spiritual growth, and tolerance
Black	Protection, stability, respect	Ridding negativity, reformation
Silver	Wisdom, intellect, memory	Spiritual development, ridding negativity, mediation
Gold	Internal strength, self-realization, understanding, instinctual increase	Success, commitment, wealth, divination
Brown	Endurance, stability, grounding, durability	Balance, focus, companion animals
Grey	Stability, neutrality, reflection	Making decisions, binding negative influences, reaching an agreement
Indigo	Emotion, insight, fluency, gracefulness	Meditation, spiritual healing, transparency of purpose
Pink	Affection, friendship, companionship	Romance, Spiritual awakening, relationships, children's magick

There are hundreds of gemstones and crystals out there to choose from. The table below consists of the most known crystals and their magical purposes in Witchcraft and Wiccan/Pagan belief.

Each crystal serves its purpose, and so when doing a ritual or a spell, make sure you choose one that works with you - not against you.

Gemstone	Properties
Amethyst	Stands for self-discipline, pride, sobriety, internal strength, peace, and self-awareness. Used for calming fears, and promote harmonious dreams and hopes. It heightens psychic abilities, increases one's true touch with themselves. It can be worn during meditation.
Tourmaline	Promotes emotional stability, break bad habits and urges, end negativity, and cleanses one's aura. It provides structure and prevents negativity from entering

	one's life. It is believed to calm the mind and body representing joy and protection internally and externally.
Citrine	Attracts warmth, happiness, and solar energies. Promotes friendship, communication, and independence.
Lapis Lazuli	Promotes truth, inner power, insight, openness, and spiritual growth. Increases intuition and helps you listen for your soul calling to guide you on your spiritual path helping you become more aware.
Moonstone	Associated with the moon, intuition and instinct, life cycles, balance, empathy, and clairvoyance. It is believed to bring someone to a deeper understanding of their feelings and what is in their heart when worn.
Quartz Crystal	This stone is worn for balance, cleansing, healing, personal power, and energy. It promotes spiritual growth and enlightenment
Rose Quartz	Promotes love, happiness, harmony, forgiveness, and understanding. Someone would wear rose quartz to boost self-confidence and reveal their inner beauty. It attracts friendships, relationships, romance, and close bonding interpersonal relationships.
Serpentine	Attracts love, luck, longevity, joy, serenity or peace, knowledge, and generosity.
Tiger's eye	Represents truth, integrity, honor, loyalty, willpower, and courage. It is associated with luck and protection. It helps someone decrease illusions, aid perceptiveness, and reveal truths. It also helps people become aware of other dishonesty and true intentions.
Turquoise	Promotes happiness, inner beauty, harmony, relaxation, and contentment. It's associated with love, prosperity, friendship, and protection. Turquoise is a stone that once worn, attunes its ability to the person wearing and increases its power focusing on where the person most needs it.

There are plenty more gemstones, each with their individual uses, which would take up an entire book. However, the crystals provided above should get you started on your path to finding what works best for you.

Herbs, Plants, and Essential Oils

Witches will use herbs, plants, and essential oils for their traditional ritual practice and spell castings. Each her, plant, or essential oil has their focus, and it is up to the individual witch on which to choose for their practice or ritual.

An herb is not a tree or a shrub, and so the term 'herb' from a witch's purpose is to define them as a plant that is useful without its regard to its lifestyle. Herbs in this sense do not include fruit, vegetables, or food purposes. The table below represents the main herbs that a witch will use in their practice.

Herbs	Magical Purposes	Uses
Cinnamon	Spiritual quests, augmenting power, love, success, healing, cleansing.	Digestive aide in tea form. Balances the gut after heavy a heavy meal or dessert. Makes a good anointing oil for a magical purpose.
Clove	Dispels negativity and bind people who speak bad of you, worn as a protective charm. Cleansing and purification	Used as an antiseptic for tooth pain and deterrent for colds; eases nausea and vomiting, and prevents disease and illness or infection
Coriander	Protecting the home, used in ritual drinks. Burnt on incenses for life longevity and love spells.	Makes a good love potion for two consenting parties. Also used in love sachets and charms.
Rose	Love, friendship, luck, protection, psychic power, and divination	Rose petals are used in honey to ease nausea and sore throats. They are high in Vitamin C
Rosemary	Improves memory, sleep, purification, youth, love, power, healing, protection, and wisdom	It is an antiseptic to wounds and can be a stimulant. Treats cases of flu reduce stress and headache or pains. Mental and physical boosters. Many benefits to rosemary.
Thyme	Sleep, psychic ability, courage, healing, purification, incense magical cleansing. and warding off negative spirits and energy.	Antibacterial, antibiotic, and diuretic properties. Treats whooping cough, warts, rheumatism, and acne. Very good for other things such as colds, flu, fevers, etc.
Pine	Attunement to nature, balance, cleansing, healing, focus, purification, fertility.	Add to bathwater to ease aches and pains or swelling. Suited for its aromatic qualities bringing balance, and enhancement to nature.
Aloe	Beauty, protection, success, peace, and harmony.	Treats wounds and maintains healthy skin. It is applied in gel form for burns and relieves rashes. It helps to combat infections and growing bacteria.

		Grow in the garden as a protection aid. Carry the root with you for protection also.
Angelica	Protection	Grow in the garden as a protection aid. Carry the root with you for protection also.
Anise	Protection, purification, awareness, and happiness	Treats coughs, bronchitis, and stuffy noses. Prevents bad dreams, relieves an upset stomach, may help with menopausal symptoms.

Here is a table of essential oils that Wiccans will use in their Witchcraft:

Essential Oil	Metaphysical Properties
Bergamot	Increases money flow into your life, and magickal energy
Carnation	Increases physical and magickal energy, and is used in magick containing health and love.
Citronella	Clear your mind of negative energies and energizes your thoughts. Protects your Sacred Circle.
Cedarwood	Promotes spirituality and deepens your link to the deity. Involves self-control
Dragon's Blood	Purification, ritual magick, love, protection, and exorcism
Eucalyptus	Heal a room or house of negative psychic energy.
Frankincense	Heightens your awareness of spiritual realms, deepens the religious experience, reduces stress, and promotes higher consciousness.
Lavender	It involves health, love, and harmony. It decreases depression and anxious feelings and also helps with sleep and relaxation.
Peppermint	Self-purification and visualization.
Vanilla	Revitalizes the body, and can be used to channel into physical exertion or magick rituals. Inhale it to promote a loving sexual relationship.

Reality Manifestation

Reality is something that is a shared dream being manifested by everyone who shares it. It is linear time which means that we start at one end of the spectrum and move to the next in which the future is an illusion.

For example, think of a river; time is not consistent, but instead, it's our consciousness that moves through numerous timelines and experiences.

Every physical thing or possibility has already manifested or exists within a static hologram. It's like the mystical Kabbalah tree, which we will use to understand reality.

The branches represent our paths, which allow us the possibilities of our experiences, in which we can choose to take to learn from our life lessons. So, like "the law of attraction" what we put out into the world will eventually come back to us.

So, if we are giving out negative energy than we will attract negativity. Whereas if we adopt a positive mindset, what we attract is positivity.

The Manifestation Limits

Eventually, it may be possible to fly, or move mountains; however, some limits limit us from doing as we want. These limits are in place for safeguards to make us understand that what can seem like an impossible task will feel more attainable. Here are the limits:

Illusory limits

These limits exist in our minds and are our insecurities and false beliefs upon your intellectual and physical capabilities. For example, if you don't believe you can pick up a car to save a life, you will not physically be able to.

Practical limits

These limits are the things you cannot do YET, such as telepathy or moving objects with your mind. Overcoming the practical limits requires you to spiritually evolve to a place where you can do these things. This can be done through knowledge and awareness.

Imposed limits

This is a limit where a higher spiritual evolved being has placed on you. This could include your higher self or your high spiritual guides. First, you must learn the necessary lessons to overcome these barriers.

Implementing a positive mindset can be the thing stopping you from overcoming the limit you are faced with. A positive mindset is not just about keeping positivity in our lives, it's also about learning how not to push away the warning signs that a lesson is trying to teach us.

There are techniques to enable our reality creation. The following is just one example:

- Present yourself with the given moment. This will anchor you with what's happening right now. Once stabilized and grounded, picture a golden flame in the center of your heart. Then imagine the light of the golden flame escalating through your body.
- Now visualize the desired reality in as much detail as you can.
- The next step is to request or partition to all higher positive aspects of your consciousness and spirit.

If you are ready and at a place where your request can be answered, your reality that you envision will come true.

This is because our desired reality aligns with our actual reality and becomes synchronized. So, we cannot just wish for something and then have it happened right away. It takes practice and patience.

Remember, what you put out into the universe should repay you threefold. This is the law of attraction.

The Theban Alphabet

The Theban alphabet is also known as the Witch's Alphabet. It is a writing system with uncertain origins that came to publication in the sixteenth century. Another name for the Theban alphabet is

"The Runes of Honorius". For the letters "j" and "u", the Theban letters are the same, and the same is true for letters "i" and "v".

This alphabet is used by witches to write their spells, inscriptions, and other important texts. People who do not know the Theban alphabet will not understand how to read it, and so it serves as a disguise to the blind eye. It also gives texts a mystical quality.

Conclusion

Did you get all your questions answered?

Which witch are you?

Which religion do you want to follow?

The purpose of this Wicca book for beginners is to help you understand Wicca and what it means to be a Wiccan. There are many benefits to practicing or joining Wicca, but unlike most religions, Wicca does not recruit members.

The purpose of this book is not to persuade you to join Wicca or dabble in Witchcraft; it simply will provide you with information and, in the end, you can do with it what you will.

One of the greatest benefits of Wiccan traditions is that the choice is always yours. You can choose what you want to participate in, which gods and goddesses to call upon, and what holidays you want to celebrate.

Other Books by Dora McGregor

Do you love Wicca? Visit Dora's Full Library following this link:

amazon.com/author/doramcgregor

Wicca for Beginners

Wiccan Traditions and Beliefs, Witchcraft Philosophy, Practical Magic, Candle, Crystals and Herbal Rituals

Wicca Moon Magic

A Wicca Grimoire on Moon Magic Power with Moon Spells and Rituals for Witchcraft Practitioners and Beginners

Wiccan Spells

A Book of Shadows for Wiccans, Witches, and Practitioners with Candle, Crystal, Herbal, Healing, Protection Spells for Beginners

Wicca Starter Kit

2 Manuscripts: Wicca for Beginner, Wiccan Spells

Made in the USA
Las Vegas, NV
24 October 2023

79603273R00080